The Apostolic Fathers

The Apostolic Fathers

A Narrative Introduction

KENNETH BERDING

May you find encouragement as you read about those who have gone before you! It's wonderful serving together with you at Biola.

Ken Berding

WIPF & STOCK · Eugene, Oregon

THE APOSTOLIC FATHERS
A Narrative Introduction

Wipf & Stock
An Imprint of Wipf and Stock Publishers
199 W. 8th Ave., Suite 3
Eugene, OR 97401

www.wipfandstock.com

PAPERBACK ISBN: 978-1-5326-1692-1
HARDCOVER ISBN: 978-1-4982-4097-0
EBOOK ISBN: 978-1-4982-4096-3

Manufactured in the U.S.A.   FEBRUARY 28, 2017

All translations of the texts of the Apostolic Fathers are original translations
by the author.

Contents

CONTENTS

Prologue

FROM THE CHURCH OF God residing as foreigners in Smyrna, to the church of God residing as foreigners in Philomelium, and to all the communities of the holy and true church residing as foreigners in every place. May the mercy, peace, and love of God the Father and our Lord Jesus Christ be multiplied to you.

We write to you, brothers and sisters, following the persecutions and martyrdoms we endured—especially the martyrdom of our blessed Polycarp—whose death was according to the gospel and who followed in the steps of our Lord Jesus Christ. Polycarp's martyrdom put an end to our recent persecutions in Smyrna. We will write about his death shortly, but first we wanted to relate to you what happened—and what he recounted—during the days before he was taken into glory.

Polycarp's final days began on the day our dear brother Germanicus courageously suffered for his Lord and entered into his rest. The crowd began taunting the Christians and shouting to the officials to get rid of the "atheists" (atheists they call us!), and to apprehend Polycarp. When the elderly Polycarp learned about the threat against him, he appeared untroubled by it. In truth, he wanted to stay in Smyrna, but the rest of the congregation persuaded him to escape the city, at least for a time. So he withdrew to a small country house not far from Smyrna and remained for less than a week with a few companions.

During those days Polycarp prayed morning and evening—and often in between—for everyone he knew and for the churches throughout the world, which was his regular practice. We were afraid that we might not have much time remaining with him, a fear that turned out to be well-founded. So we took every opportunity to dialogue with our dear bishop about his many years of ministry and anything else we could think to ask him about the church of our Lord Jesus Christ during his lifetime and before. We learned some information we hadn't previously heard, though Polycarp has always been faithful to transmit what he received. It was a priceless gift to listen while he recounted the history of God's church, and especially to hear his reflections on the documents that have been written in the decades since the apostles passed into glory. Following is an account of our conversations with the blessed Polycarp during the week we hid out together in the country. This account is based upon the collective memories of the four who were appointed by the church of Smyrna to care for him during the final days before his glorious exodus.

Main Characters: There are four main characters besides Polycarp in this story:

Bourrus: About sixty years old, owner of the country house where Polycarp hid out, an elder in the church in Smyrna.

Rufina: Bourrus's wife, in her upper-forties, and co-owner of the country house.

Tavia: A deaconess of the church in Smyrna, in her early thirties, and cook for the group.

Artemidorus: A young man about twenty years old, Polycarp's regular assistant, and a relatively new Christian.

There are also a few minor characters in the story:

Crocus: Polycarp's great nephew, not a believer, courier of goods and information between Smyrna and the group hiding in the country house.

Anthousa: Christian slave girl #1.

Alce: Christian slave girl #2.

See pages 107–108 for why these names were chosen for these characters. Refer to the Historical and Literary Notes on pages 105–139 to sort out what is historical from what is fictional in the narrative.

Chapter 1

The Period of the Apostolic Fathers
Monday Morning

"Good morning, Tavia. I hope you slept well."

"Good morning, Polycarp. Would you like some breakfast?"

"Thank you, if it isn't too difficult for you."

"It's already prepared. The others are waiting in the courtyard."

Polycarp shuffled toward a shaded courtyard enclosed by walls on all sides. "Good morning, precious friends."

"Good morning, Polycarp," replied a slightly balding man. Bourrus, who had known Polycarp for almost four decades, added, "But please, Polycarp, speak quietly. No one can know you're here."

"Yes, of course. I will try. But you know, I've been preaching for so long—and when you factor in my hearing-loss—I'm afraid that you may have to remind me once in a while."

"Did you get any sleep?" queried Rufina, wife of Bourrus and co-owner of the house where the five were hiding.

"Yes, I slept well enough, thank you, Rufina, although . . . I think I may have some bruises on my back side from our middle-of-the-night journey out of Smyrna!"

"A midnight journey really was necessary." Artemidorus, Polycarp's broad-shouldered young assistant and self-appointed bodyguard spoke up. "We were concerned that we might be followed if we traveled during the day. It was fortunate that the clouds mostly hid the moon, but it also made it difficult to avoid the dips in the road. I wish we could have brought you out on something more comfortable than a donkey."

"It's not a problem, really," Polycarp replied. "I'm thankful for how well all of you have taken care of me."

"We're glad to do so," replied the deaconess Tavia. Tavia was in her early thirties and known for her interest in Christian doctrine and the way she graciously served others. She also was the only person in the group who knew how to cook. "But we have to be careful. It's one thing to get you here without being seen; it's quite another to keep the neighbors from finding out about you, even if the closest farm house is some distance down the road."

"I'm ready to die for Christ."

"Yes, we know," replied Artemidorus, "But you agreed to let us bring you out to this country house, at least until things calm down in the city. And, please, can you. . . . "

"I'll try to keep my voice down."

"Thank you."

"Brother Polycarp," inquired Bourrus. "The four of us have been talking—and we would like to ask a favor of you."

"Yes, of course. Whatever I can do . . . You've already done so much for me."

"We know that your plan while you're here is to spend a lot of time in prayer for the Christians in Smyrna and for the churches around the world, but we were wondering whether you might be gracious enough to allow us to use some of our morning and evening meals to hear your memories from the past and learn some of what you have acquired over the years about the church of Jesus Christ throughout the world."

"I'm not dead yet!"

"No, of course not, dear Polycarp," interjected the middle-aged Rufina, "but since you have lived so much longer than the rest of us, we were hoping to glean whatever wisdom you might choose to impart to us from your long and spiritually rich life."

"The fear of the Lord is the beginning of wisdom; that's a good place to start. And, yes, I am old—that I'll grant—and I can't move fast anymore. But that's why turtles live so long—because they move so slowly!" Polycarp chuckled at his analogy.

"So you're willing to share some of your memories with us?" Tavia asked eagerly.

"I'd be glad to encourage you in any way I can. If talking about the past is a way to accomplish that, then I am eager to share what I know. There is nothing I'd enjoy more than conversing about the things God has done in his church while I break bread with four treasured friends. Since this appears to be our plan, where shall we begin?"

Bourrus—the oldest member of the group-of-four appointed by the church of Smyrna to look after Polycarp, and an elder of that church—spoke for all. "Would you mind sharing with us your greatest joys—as well as some of the difficulties you've encountered—during your many years serving Christ?"

"My greatest joy . . . " Polycarp paused momentarily to reflect, " . . . is that I was introduced to the good news in my youth by apostles and other disciples who had known Jesus. The godly examples, faithful transmission of the message, and courageous deaths of many of those early followers of Jesus have been a constant reminder to me of the calling I received from Jesus Christ my Savior. I still cannot get over how much grace has been bestowed on me by my Lord.

"Probably my second greatest joy has been to observe the miracle of the spread of the gospel of Christ to so many regions during my lifetime. When I was young there were only a few, and—with occasional exceptions—mostly small communities of disciples connected to such cities as Jerusalem, Antioch, Corinth, Rome, and, of course, some of the cities of our own province of Asia. But as you know, Christians these days who pass through Smyrna keep bringing reports of new communities springing up—almost every day, it seems—in such places as Alexandria, Carthage, Gaul, and Spain. What gives me joy? Knowing that Jesus Christ is being proclaimed—in this I rejoice, as the blessed Paul wrote. And I will rejoice!"

Rufina started to speak, paused, and then gently probed, "But you also have experienced many heartaches and difficulties during your lifetime, have you not, Polycarp?"

"Indeed I have." Polycarp grew somber. The Christians who have suffered for their faithful testimony remind me of the cost of following Christ. There were dreadful torments in Rome during Nero's reign of terror—although I did not live through them I have heard many stories—and various regional persecutions, including the loss of life of eleven of our own from Smyrna and Philadelphia. How much I miss Germanicus . . . and the others! But I remember the words of our Lord when he said, 'Blessed are those who are persecuted for the sake of righteousness, for theirs is the kingdom of God.'

"I also feel a deep sadness for how few Jewish brothers and sisters there are in our midst anymore. We are all part of one body, but these days the increasing numbers of Gentiles in our churches have almost displaced the Jewish influence. When I was young, some house churches were, of course, entirely Jewish—or for that matter, entirely another ethnicity—but I still remember how many groups were thoroughly integrated. That afforded many challenges, and no shortage of tensions, but I still remember those days fondly and grieve our loss of fellowship. We still combine our various ethnicities as one body in Christ, but there are now so few Jews who accept Jesus as Messiah that it feels as though we've lost an arm or a leg. More challenging yet is that the handful of Jewish brothers and sisters among us are no longer permitted access to their synagogues. The gap between Christian society and ethnic Israel seems almost too wide to bridge anymore. It wasn't always that way."

Bourrus interjected, "It doesn't help that the Jewish community in Smyrna is unhappy with our Christian groups."

"I know . . . and that grieves me deeply. To further confuse matters is the existence of Jewish groups who claim to follow Jesus, but who hold views distinct from Christians and Jews alike. Doubtless the Jewish community in Smyrna has heard about such groups, even though the poor–ones are mostly found in or near Palestine."

"The poor–ones? I've never heard of them," said Artemidorus.

"They refer to themselves this way, perhaps because Jesus taught that the kingdom of heaven belongs to those who are poor. Actually, I don't really know why they are called poor–ones. They claim to believe in Jesus like we do, but they deny his divinity. They assert that Jesus was born human through the natural and physical union of Joseph and Mary. They think that Jesus was declared to be Messiah by God because he was righteous and followed the Law so well. So they press for the observance of traditions. They also dislike the writings of the Apostle Paul; they think he was an imposter."

"That must be confusing to the Jewish community. But the poor ones haven't been among your primary adversaries, have they, Polycarp?" Bourrus asked leadingly.

"No they haven't. Since you asked it, Bourrus, who do *you* think my most trying opponents have been?" Polycarp looked over at the one-time traveling companion and scribe of Ignatius and his own long–time protégé with respect and gratefulness.

"I'd be astonished if you didn't bring up the 'knowing–ones.' Am I right?"

"Indeed you are."

When Bourrus mentioned the knowing–ones, Polycarp glanced in the direction of Rufina, who blushed slightly. "Yes, many have been attracted by the promise of higher knowledge. Since the creation of humans, the desire to be *in the know* has been too powerful for many to resist."

Rufina decided to enter the conversation, despite her history. "The appeal of higher knowledge is strong. There is a feeling of power in secret understanding, and a sense of belonging when you're one of the special ones who *know*."

"I don't *know* what you're talking about," exclaimed Artemidorus. The others smiled at his quip. "Can someone please tell me what you're talking about?"

Rufina replied, "Apparently you haven't heard that about twelve years ago—despite having been a Christian already for a long time—I got caught up for most of a year with some professing Christians who were promoting the teaching of Valentinus."

"Oh . . . I didn't know you were . . . "

"Bourrus and I argued a lot that year." She glanced over at her husband who nodded in agreement. "I was told by people who claimed to be Christians that the highest God had placed a spark of the divine in me and that he wanted to redeem me from this evil world. The Creator of our world, on the other hand—an emanation of an emanation of an emanation of the highest God, that is, a different God altogether—either wanted me to suffer or didn't care if I did. Our world is evil, since it was created by this 'Demiurge,' as they call him, and we need release. They claimed that Christ came into the world to redeem us, not by dying in his body on the cross; that would be impossible, they said, since he couldn't do that in an evil body. They taught that Christ came into the world as a spirit who entered into Jesus at baptism. He used Jesus' mouth to teach that some could get released from the entrapment of this world through special knowledge of the past, and thus help them prepare to travel after their deaths through the dangerous demonic upper spheres to reunite with the highest God. According to what they told me, after Jesus imparted knowledge of the cosmic past and explained to his disciples how to negotiate their future journeys after death, the spirit–Christ abandoned Jesus to suffer his death alone."

"And you got pulled in by *that*?" asked Artemidorus.

Rufina hesitated. "I'm not proud of it."

Polycarp intervened, "You see, my young brother, the reason that the knowing–ones have been so difficult during these past years—more so than any others except perhaps the followers of Marcion—is that they still think of themselves as Christians—just more knowledgeable ones—and so keep hanging around our churches. There are various streams of this false teaching, but a common idea among the knowing–ones is that there are three kinds of people in the world: the basic people created by the Demiurge who possess neither spirit nor future possibilities, normal

Christians who simply believe in Christ, and spiritual Christians like themselves who possess a secret, higher knowledge. So they keep coming to our meetings with the hope of enticing those who are weak and untrained to look into their special knowledge. But the knowledge they advocate is a peculiar mixture of Christian doctrine and other ideas drawn from various religious systems."

"What about Marcion? He teaches that there is more than one God as well, right?" inquired Artemidorus.

"Marcion . . . " Polycarp grew severe at the mention of his name. "Marcion claims that the idea that there is only one God is inadequate to explain God's severity, so at least in this way he is similar to the knowing-ones. Marcion describes the God of the Old Covenant like a harsh and exacting judge—and then contrasts that God with the God of the New Covenant whom he views as a God of love. But Marcion doesn't have time for all the mythological nonsense of the knowing–ones and their elaborate ideas about multiple divine beings—and so differs in many ways from them."

"He also rejects the writings of Moses and the Prophets, not to mention many of the apostles' writings," said Bourrus.

"That's right . . . because those writings in his view are about a merciless God who differs decidedly from the benevolent God described in Paul's writings," added Polycarp. "So when Marcion needs authority to back up his claims, he usually draws upon the writings of the Apostle Paul or the teachings of Jesus according to Luke, even though he regularly distorts them. Marcion and his followers pose a constant risk for our younger brothers and sisters. Sometimes I wonder if they are more dangerous than the knowing–ones. The knowing–ones hang around our gatherings—often without telling us their beliefs—looking for people to recruit. The followers of Marcion brazenly challenge us by starting their own assemblies with their own leadership structures and by living rigorously moral lives that appeal to some of our newer believers."

Artemidorus interjected, "I've heard, Polycarp, that you said something . . . umm . . . interesting when you met Marcion face to face. Is the report true?"

Polycarp laughed. "Yes, it's true. When Marcion walked up to me and asked if I knew who he was, I looked him in the eye and responded: 'I know you, the first-born of Satan.'"

"Why did you call him that?" asked Artemidorus.

"Because the apostles warned us against associating with so-called brothers who teach falsehood. Besides, Marcion's movement is growing rapidly. Fewer than twenty years have passed since he showed up in Rome, and even during his first few years in Rome he kept his views under wraps for a time. When he first arrived in Rome, he donated the enormous sum of 200,000 sesterces for the church's mission. As a result he seems to have assumed that his donation would give him some sort of platform to spread his views. But once he started actively disseminating teachings contrary to the standards of our tradition, the church leaders in Rome expelled him from the church and returned all his money. But that wasn't about to stop him, since he sincerely believed he was right. Recently, he's been traveling around Asia founding new churches—not real churches, mind you, nor even churches primarily comprised of former pagans—but churches largely full of people who used to be in our churches, who now have been persuaded of his views."

At this comment everyone became quiet as they recalled friends and former members of their Christian community who had broken off fellowship because they had decided to identify with Marcion and his false doctrine. A tear even worked its way down Polycarp's cheek, but Polycarp knew what to do. After so many years living through on-and-off persecutions at the hands of Roman magistrates, tensions with the Jewish community, false teaching introduced by the knowing-ones and the followers of Marcion, Polycarp knew where to go and what to do. He had learned it from those who had learned it from Jesus. Polycarp looked around at four people he deeply loved and quietly suggested, "Let us pray for a while." And so they did.

Chapter 2

First Clement

Monday Evening

"Is there any word from Crocus?" asked Polycarp as he hobbled toward the table. "Wasn't his plan to show up with some extra supplies . . . books and food?"

"Books first? Really, Polycarp . . . " retorted Artemidorus. "Shouldn't food always come first? As for Crocus, maybe he didn't want to travel while the sun was still up. It would be unfortunate if he led the authorities to you."

"Maybe they're not even looking for me," countered Polycarp. "Just because people shouted my name in the stadium doesn't mean the authorities will follow up on their taunt. Perhaps this storm will blow over soon and I can get back to doing regular ministry in Smyrna."

"We wouldn't have brought you here if there wasn't real danger," spoke Rufina gently.

"I know," responded Polycarp. "And I'm deeply grateful. But I want to be faithful and finish the ministry I've been assigned by the Lord Jesus. It's difficult to do that while hiding out in the country."

"You can minister to us!" countered Tavia. "Don't forget, we want to learn from you."

"Yes, I can do that," Polycarp replied warmly. "I'm glad to be sharing this time with the four of you."

Bourrus added. "Don't worry, Polycarp, the other leaders are capable of caring for the flock while we are on this . . . nice . . . holiday."

"Yes, undoubtedly they are able. Not every church shares the same unity with one another that we possess in Smyrna."

"Are you thinking of something specific?" inquired Tavia.

"Actually, this morning I was praying for the church in Corinth. I couldn't help but remember the dissension in that church, and how the church leaders in Rome intervened. But that was a long time ago, long before you were born."

"Please talk to us about it," entreated Tavia. "This is the type of conversation we're all hoping to have with you."

"Well," started Polycarp, "I was a young man engaged in ministry when I first heard unsettling reports coming out of Corinth. I was energetic and highly motivated to see God's kingdom spread to more and more people." Polycarp looked over at the young man sitting beside him. "I was like you, Artemidorus, faithful, zealous, willing—but still needing significant maturing." Artemidorus accepted Polycarp's admonition.

The elderly man continued, "Since ships regularly traverse the Aegean between Corinth and Smyrna—it's only a few days' journey by ship, as you know—we kept getting updates from the believers who passed through. First there were rumblings that young men in the congregation weren't happy with the way the Corinthian church was being run by the elders, and that they wanted to try some new methods. Remember, I was a young man myself, and I'd had some of those same thoughts about the ministry in Smyrna. I was curious to hear how things developed in Corinth. But I wasn't prepared for what happened next."

"What happened?" asked Artemidorus.

"There was a revolt. The young men, up-and-coming leaders, decided that their complaints weren't being heard by the established elders and took matters into their own hands. The church in Corinth had continued to grow since the time Paul had founded it. This meant that a majority of believers in Corinth were young. The younger leaders, therefore, had little trouble convincing the majority of the congregants that the church needed to start moving in a different direction. Of course, there were some who didn't want a change in leadership, but they were in the minority. The elders did everything they could to persuade the impetuous young men to stop their rebellion—and urged the newer believers not to listen to them or follow them—but to no avail. It was a contentious and factious period in Corinth. In the end, the older leaders lost the confidence of the various house churches, and the majority started following the self-appointed leaders.

"As for me, I was initially intrigued by the proposals of the younger men, but quickly changed my opinion when I heard about their aggressive takeover. Even though I agreed that some new approaches in our mission to the world should be tried, I knew that rejecting the elders, some of whom had been appointed by apostles, was the wrong way to go about it. The church in Corinth was founded by Paul, and although some of the elders who had known Paul had died, there were still a few around who had lived through a similar revolt during the time of Paul—and they remembered it with shame.

"I had a chance to talk about my concerns with the older leaders in Smyrna. I so appreciated their advice! They counseled me to devote myself to prayer, seek faithfulness in the place God had planted me—in Smyrna where I was starting to carry some responsibility—and trust in our sovereign Lord to work things out within the church that God himself had established. In fact, God did work it out in Corinth."

"How was that?" Tavia asked.

"It happened through the leadership of the church in Rome. When they found out about what was happening in Corinth, they were—as were we in the east—grieved over the loss of unity in one of the ancient churches. So the Roman church leaders resolved to write an urgent appeal to the young usurpers, and entreat them to repent of their ways, return the reins of leadership to the elders, and receive whatever discipline the congregation might decide for them, even if that entailed a time of 'exile' away from the congregation. The leadership in Rome also decided to send a delegation of a couple of their own elders to try to turn around the situation in Corinth."

"Why that course of action? Was the Roman church trying to exert authority over the church in Corinth?" asked Rufina.

"No, sixty years ago things were different than they are now," replied Polycarp. "The church in Rome wasn't led by a governing bishop who directed the affairs of all the house groups in his own city—much less who directed the affairs of people outside of Rome. Leadership in those days was exercised by a group of elders, and their leadership was limited to the city of Rome and its immediate environs. The church in Rome simply didn't have influence over churches at a distance like they sometimes try to exercise now."

Bourrus interjected, "But, Polycarp, even today Bishop Anicetus in Rome can't enforce his will on churches outside of Rome. Your recent expedition to Rome illustrates this better than anything else. Our churches in the province of Asia celebrate the death and resurrection of Jesus on Nisan 14 in conjunction with the Jewish Passover, on whichever day of the week it happens to fall. But the Roman bishop insists that the resurrection of Jesus should always be celebrated on a Sunday since Jesus was resurrected on Sunday. Even though Anicetus wanted everyone in the world to follow the Roman practice, he couldn't persuade you or the delegation from the churches of Asia to fall in line with his position."

"I'm glad you stood your ground!" cheered Artemidorus.

Polycarp ignored the young man. "You're right, Bourrus. The church in Rome cannot enforce their will upon the churches in our region. Our churches are still strong and growing, and continue to be well-connected to Christians throughout the world, but today the church in Rome is increasing in influence and exercises more sway than any other church. But sixty years ago it wasn't that way. Leadership was still local and shared by a group of elders."

"I'm confused, Polycarp. What about Clement? Wasn't he the bishop of the Roman church during those days?" asked Rufina. "I thought the letter sent to Corinth from Rome was written by bishop Clement."

"It is true that the letter was penned by Clement, a leading elder in the church in Rome, though it really isn't accurate to view the letter simply as his own work. Nor would it be accurate to refer to him as a bishop, at least not if we mean the same thing by the word 'bishop' that we mean when we use that word now. From our vantage point, it is easy to look back sixty years and think of Clement as a bishop over the whole city of Rome, since that's what the word bishop has come to mean, but that wasn't how churches were organized then. Clement was at that time a leading elder among a group of elders who oversaw the affairs of the church in Rome. The next time you get an opportunity to look at the letter itself—maybe it will be among the books Crocus brings when he shows up—you'll see that the letter that now bears his name repeatedly uses the words 'we' and 'us' instead of the word 'I'. So even though Clement penned the letter, the influence and agreement of the Roman leaders is behind everything he wrote. The letter presents a unified front from beginning to end, starting with the words 'The church of God sojourning in Rome to the church of God sojourning in Corinth'—not 'Clement to the church in Corinth'—and it ends with 'The letter of the Romans to the Corinthians.'"

"So if the church leaders in Rome didn't think they could exercise authority over the church in Corinth, why did they decide to send the letter in the first place?" asked Rufina.

"They were trying to persuade them—not command them—to submit to the will of God and stop their rebellion. Note that the letter calls upon Christians in Corinth to submit to the will of God; they do not call on them to submit to the will of the Roman church leadership. The tone of the letter is full of persuasion, not directives."

"That makes more sense to me now. So if Clement was trying to persuade them rather than command them to do what was right, what form did his persuasion take?" asked Rufina.

Polycarp explained, "Clement started his persuasion by mentioning Christian qualities that had formerly characterized the Corinthian church: their faith, piety, hospitality, and knowledge. He reminded them of the order and unity with which they had carried out their church affairs. But encouragement wasn't his goal in this letter; his goal was to convince them to stop their jealousy, fighting, and rebellion.

"He did this early in the letter by reminding them of negative examples of envy and fighting from the past: Cain toward Abel, Esau toward Jacob, Saul toward David. He also appealed to positive examples from the more recent past of Paul and Peter, and of women who suffered injustice with patient endurance. The use of positive types from the past was one of the primary ways Clement—and the elders in Rome along with him—sought to persuade the Corinthians: Noah, Jonah, Abraham, Lot, and Rahab; prophets like Elijah, Elisha, and Ezekiel; Job, David, Moses, and Esther, among so many others. If such heroes of the faith strove for harmony, then certainly the Christians in Corinth ought to endeavor to do the same.

"Another way Clement sought to persuade the Corinthians was by appealing to the natural order. He pointed out the way the stars in the sky move in agreement, the regularity of the seasons, the seas and the winds, and used such examples to argue that there should be harmony in the church.

"Furthermore, Clement encouraged a response by appealing to the teaching that had been passed down from the apostles—referring to it as 'the rule of our tradition' that was handed down to them—and by calling upon the Corinthians to conform to it. He quoted larger sections of Scripture to substantiate his points, whether from the Psalms, from the narrative about Job, or from the Proverbs. Perhaps most significant—and different in this way from Ignatius of Antioch—is that Clement appealed to a line of succession that started with Jesus and continued to his day. Jesus appointed the apostles, and the apostles appointed leaders in their churches, both bishops and deacons. Since Corinth could boast an unbroken line of tradition from the apostles to the present, Clement's point was that the young usurpers ought to stop their rebellion and submit to their God–appointed leaders.

"One more way he sought to persuade them was by directly connecting to the Apostle Paul's own warnings from forty years before in a letter Paul had written to them about schism. Both the church in Rome and the church in Corinth had copies of that important letter, so Clement decided to appeal to it. *Didn't Paul write you a letter in the past? Didn't Paul in that letter reprimand you for splitting into factions where some followed him, some followed Cephas, and some followed Apollos? But at least they were apostles! Who is it that you're following?"*

Bourrus remarked, "Polycarp, you haven't said anything about how *long* this letter is. I think it's one of the longest letters I've ever seen."

"Yes. I forgot to mention that. Its length alone makes you want to repent! It's as if Clement was trying to make the Corinthians feel remorse for what they had done by pointing out their mistakes in a hundred different ways! On the other hand, the letter's length is one of the things that makes it so special. It is packed full of godly and wise counsel, often on topics that don't directly connect with the conflict in Corinth, including explications of the character of God, repeated mentions of the life, death, and resurrection of Jesus, a discourse on Christian ministry, and many, many comments on general Christian living. Clement also penned a beautiful and compelling prayer toward the end of the letter, a prayer I have used repeatedly when I have needed help in my own prayers."

"Was there any response to the letter?" asked Rufina. "Did it make any difference in the church in Corinth?"

"It certainly did. The two older mediators from Rome, Claudius Ephebus and Valerius Bito, as well as a younger man named Fortunatus, were able to reason with the Corinthians and persuaded many to place themselves under the older leadership whom God had appointed for them. The church ended up having to expel a couple of the troublemakers, but the Christians in Corinth recovered from it."

"Thank you for telling us about this event and letter, Polycarp," said Rufina. We should have more discussions of this kind as long as we're hiding out here. Maybe tomorrow?"

"I'd be happy for more of these talks," replied Polycarp. "I do think, however, that it may be time to retire to my room to receive one of God's greatest gifts to humans, the gift of sleep. Goodnight, dear souls."

Excerpts from First Clement

Because of a series of misfortunes and accidents that suddenly happened to us, brothers and sisters, we admit that we have been rather slow in turning our attention to the issues in dispute among you. We are referring, beloved, to the terrible and unholy split—so foreign and strange to God's elect—which a few reckless and self-willed people have kindled to such a level of insanity that your name, previously well-known and loved by all, has been severely disgraced. (1.1)

Therefore, let us obey his magnificent and glorious will, and let us fall down before him as petitioners of his mercy and kindness. Let us return to his compassion and give up our useless efforts and fighting, and the jealousy that leads to death. Let us fix our attention on those who have perfectly served his magnificent glory. Let us take as an example Enoch, who because he was found righteous in his obedience, was taken up and never experienced death. Noah was faithful in his ministry and proclaimed a second birth to the world, and through him the Master saved the living creatures that entered peacefully into the ark. (9.1–4)

Our apostles knew through our Lord Jesus Christ that there would be jealousy over the naming of a bishop. So for this reason, because they had been given full foreknowledge, they appointed those previously mentioned and afterward made it continuous so that even if they should die, other approved men would succeed to their ministry. In light of this, we consider it unjust to remove from their ministry those who were appointed either by them or, later on, by other reputable men with the consent of the whole church, who have blamelessly ministered to the flock of Christ humbly, quietly, and unselfishly, and who have long been approved by everyone. (44.1–3)

So then, let us ask for forgiveness for falling away and for whatever we have done through the influence of the adversary. And those who have become the leaders of the revolt and dissension ought to notice the hope we have in common. For those who walk in fear and love would rather suffer mistreatment themselves than have their neighbors do so, and would rather bring condemnation upon themselves than have it fall upon the harmony that has been so well and righteously handed down to us. For it is better for a person to confess his wrongdoings than to harden his heart the way those who rebelled against Moses the servant of God hardened theirs. Their condemnation became clear. For they went down to Hades alive, and death will be their shepherd. Pharaoh and his army and all the rulers of Egypt—the chariots and their riders—were sunk into the sea for no other reason than that their foolish hearts were hardened after signs and wonders were done in the land of Egypt by God's servant Moses. (51.1–5)

Chapter 3

The Letters of Ignatius
Tuesday Morning

"Hello, Uncle Polycarp."

"Good morning, Crocus! When did you arrive?"

"About an hour ago. I wanted to be here before the sun came up." The twenty year old grand–nephew of Polycarp had been standing and talking quietly with the others in the courtyard when Polycarp came out. Crocus was gnawing on a hunk of bread.

"Any news from Smyrna?" asked Polycarp.

"They're looking for you."

"Who's looking for me?"

"Herod and all his men."

"Someone named *Herod* is looking for me?"

"The new chief constable."

"Oh." Polycarp smiled unexpectedly then said, "Isn't it curious that someone named Herod wants to talk to me? Jesus would be proud. I wonder what John the baptizer would think."

"I don't think you should make light of it, Uncle Polycarp. This is serious. And I'm afraid . . . that is, I'm afraid for . . . you."

Polycarp replied lovingly, "Crocus, there is no fear in love, but perfect love casts out fear."

"I don't believe your religious writings, Uncle. You know that."

"Then why bother helping us . . . ?" cut in Artemidorus, " . . . if you don't even believe?"

"I *am* family after all," Crocus snapped back. "I care that my grandmother's brother stays safe, and I'm concerned about the honor of the family."

Polycarp interrupted the exchange. "Crocus, I so appreciate all you're doing. You're the perfect person to act as our courier since you can keep me connected with the family, and you know so many people in the church, too. Besides, I don't think Artemidorus meant anything by it." He glanced in the direction of Artemidorus.

"Maybe not . . . " replied Artemidorus, not too convincingly.

Crocus paused for a moment. "I need to get back to the city. Uncle Polycarp, do you have any messages for me to carry?"

"Tell everyone that I'm well, and remind the Christians that they need to stay devoted to prayer during this trying period. By the way, did you bring any books with you?"

"I'm afraid not, Uncle. My bags were already full of basic supplies. Sorry about that. I'll be sure to let everyone know that you're in good spirits."

"And don't forget to remind the believers to stay devoted to prayer . . . "

"Yes, and that too."

"I appreciate what you're doing, Crocus. Thank you again, my young nephew." Crocus nodded to Polycarp and left quickly.

As soon as he was out the door, Artemidorus exclaimed, "Really, Polycarp? Why Crocus? He's not even a believer!"

"It's alright, Artemidorus. I'm glad he's willing to do this for us."

Bourrus interjected, "Yes, Crocus is the right person for the job . . . "

"We've known him since he was a baby," added Rufina.

"All the same, I'd rather our connections to Smyrna came through a Christian brother," spouted Artemidorus. "And, Polycarp, I really wish you weren't so relaxed about the predicament you're in!"

"What would you have me do, my young friend? Worry? Would my situation—or yours for that matter—improve if I started to get anxious? No, I prefer to keep trusting the Lord, the one who has faithfully led me all these years. You know I'm ready to give my life for Christ."

Artemidorus decided that now was the time to ask the question he had been mulling over, "You're not thinking of giving yourself up to the authorities, are you, Polycarp?"

"No. I have actively discouraged others from doing that and I have no plans to do it myself. Quintus rashly offered himself for martyrdom—and persuaded others to do the same—but when he got an up–close look at the dreadful beasts, the proconsul was able to coax him away from his intentions. He swore the oath to Caesar, and he offered the sacrifice to secure his release. I won't invite martyrdom like Quintus did. In this respect I'm also not like the blessed Ignatius either, though I aspire to be like him in so many other ways." When he mentioned Ignatius, Polycarp glanced over at Bourrus, but didn't address him.

Instead Tavia entreated, "Tell us about Ignatius, Polycarp. I know a little of his story, but I think there's a lot more to it I haven't heard."

"Gladly, sister Tavia," replied Polycarp, "but Bourrus knew Ignatius too, so I'll need his help in the retelling."

Tavia said, "Fine with me. But first, what did you mean by not planning to be like Ignatius 'in this way'? What 'way' were you talking about?"

Polycarp said, "Ignatius wanted to die. He was overly zealous to be thrown to the wild beasts as a Christian. Nevertheless, he still was an example of faithful suffering for Christ, and the testimony of his endurance resonates to this day. But that comes later in the story. Let's back up and start at the beginning, at least as far as our connection to Ignatius goes."

"I'd love that," said Tavia.

"Ignatius was serving the Lord in Syria and leading the church in Antioch when he was arrested," began Polycarp. "Ten Roman soldiers embarked on their long and arduous assignment

to transport the captive to Rome for execution. Ignatius lovingly—
or perhaps not so lovingly—referred to these soldiers as 'leopards'!
He was fond of metaphors, you see. He wasn't so worried that he
might get eaten by lions in the Coliseum; quite the opposite in fact
. . . But he was apprehensive about possible turmoil back in the
church in Antioch now that they were bereft of their leader."

"When the company of soldiers and prisoners neared our
region," Bourrus picked up the story, "they adjusted their travel
plans away from the southern route that would have passed near
Tralles, Magnesia, and Ephesus, and instead headed north, first
through Philadelphia and then on to Smyrna."

"That's where my husband came into the story," interjected
Rufina in a tone that betrayed her admiration for Bourrus. "The
three churches south of Smyrna had heard that Ignatius was on the
way and were preparing for his arrival. After the southern churches received news that the company of soldiers—and Ignatius along
with them—had veered north, the church in Ephesus dispatched
a group of representatives to intercept Ignatius in Smyrna. The
delegation included their bishop Onesimus, my eventual husband
Bourrus, and a man named Crocus."

"Oh, like our Crocus," remarked Tavia.

"But *he* was a believer," retorted Artemidorus.

Ignoring Artemidorus, Bourrus picked up the story. "There
were also others who came to Smyrna hoping to see Ignatius, including Damas from Magnesia and Polybius from Tralles. The soldiers rested in Smyrna for a few days before resuming their march.
They allowed Ignatius to meet the delegates from the southern
churches and to spend some time with Polycarp and a few other
Christians from Smyrna. During those days Ignatius dictated letters to the churches on the southern route—one letter each for the
Ephesians, the Magnesians, and the Trallians—in addition to one
letter to Rome."

"What are those letters about?" asked Tavia.

"The letters to the three churches south of Smyrna are full
of helpful Christian exhortations and warnings against false
teaching," replied Polycarp. "But Ignatius's primary concern was

that people should meticulously obey their bishop. In Ignatius's view, the best way for a Christian to obey God was by obeying the bishop God had placed over him. Ignatius wanted everything that a Christian did—and I think Ignatius meant just about everything—to be done under the leadership of the bishop."

"What about the letter to Rome? What was different about that?" asked Artemidorus.

"The letter to the church in that great city has a different feel than Ignatius's other letters, and was written with a different purpose. Ignatius dictated a heart–wrenching entreaty to the Christians in Rome, begging them not to use any clout they might possess in an attempt to prevent him from being thrown to the wild beasts. Ignatius was fixated on his death in that letter. Parts of the letter to the Romans are difficult to read because of the graphic details he used to describe his anticipated fate."

"So, that's what you meant about not being like Ignatius in a certain way," said Tavia.

"That's correct. Ignatius took it even further, though. In his letter to Rome—as well as in a couple of his others letters—he made an unusual claim. He alleged that only after he had become a prisoner on his way to execution did he really start to become a disciple. I think he really was an exemplary disciple before then, but he viewed his captivity on the way to martyrdom as making him a disciple in some special sense."

Bourrus spoke, "After a few days in Smyrna, the soldiers resumed their march north, pausing again when we arrived in Troas. I say 'we' because I was with them. It was a hard march, and I will never forget it. I had been appointed by the leaders of Ephesus and Smyrna to travel with Ignatius on the next leg of his arduous journey and help him in any way I could. I joined Rhaius Agathopus who had been with Ignatius on the entire journey from Syria, and Philo who had been traveling with Ignatius since Cilicia."

Rufina explained, "The elders chose Bourrus because he was an excellent scribe."

"Ignatius was hoping to dispatch more letters," added Bourrus. "Surprisingly, a precious gift in the form of good news was waiting for him when he arrived in Troas. Word had reached Troas just before we arrived that God had answered Ignatius's worried prayers for peace to be restored to his church in Antioch. He learned that the turmoil in Antioch had died down, and that the church was united. Ignatius was deeply moved by this news. The bishop of Antioch had been intensely concerned about how his flock might fare in the absence of their shepherd.

"Our company planned to pause for a couple days in Troas like we had in Smyrna, so Ignatius dictated three letters, one for the church in Philadelphia—since he had overnighted there before he arrived in Smyrna—one for the church in Smyrna, and one for Polycarp, adding up to seven letters in all that he composed on his way to Rome. Ignatius asked the churches in Asia to send representatives back to Antioch to encourage the believers there. I wrote all this down for Ignatius.

"When the squad leader discovered that a ship was about to sail for Neapolis, Ignatius instructed me to stay, write up final drafts and a copy of each letter, and travel back to Smyrna and Philadelphia to deliver them. I headed back to Smyrna with two letters in hand for that city and then over to Philadelphia to deliver their letter, and thus completed the task assigned to me."

Polycarp remarked, "Ignatius's letter to me, as well as his exhortations to the church in my city, helped strengthen my leadership role in Smyrna. By that time I was the lead elder in the city, but Ignatius's urgings about the importance of a single governing bishop to protect the churches against false doctrine made an impact on future leadership arrangements in Smyrna. Ignatius emphasized obedience to the bishop in all his letters except his letter to Rome. So Ignatius's appeals also strengthened the hands of Onesimus in Ephesus, though he was already pretty well–established there, of Damas in Magnesia, though he was probably too young to be in that role, of Polybius in Tralles, and also of the quiet bishop of Philadelphia." Polycarp exchanged a knowing smile with Bourrus as the two of them remembered the leader of Philadelphia whom Ignatius claimed accomplished more with his silence than others do with words.

"Ignatius treated us in his letters as though we were already governing bishops, and wanted us to exercise the kind of authority I have from God in Smyrna today—or the kind of authority Ignatius was trying to exert in Antioch before his arrest. But don't forget that this was a period of transition, and the system of governing bishops was not functioning everywhere yet; that's why Ignatius pressed his point so strongly in his letters. You'll notice when you read his letter to the Roman church that Ignatius doesn't address a bishop at all. But Ignatius made an excellent case when he argued that a governing bishop is the best person to protect a church from false doctrine, not to mention that the bishop is usually the wisest one to guide in Christian ethics. A bishop who adheres to and teaches the deposit of Christian teaching can protect his flock from the infiltration of false doctrine and ungodly practice like no one else can. Who is better to guide the daily decisions of one's life than a devout bishop? That is why he pressed so hard for obedience to the bishop in his letters. Ignatius's point made its mark on our churches."

"What kinds of false teaching was Ignatius worried about?" asked Tavia, the deaconess who was so interested in Christian doctrine. "What were his main concerns during that period?"

Polycarp replied, "There were two kinds of false teaching that Ignatius was most concerned about. In his letters to the Magnesians and the Philadelphians he seemed most apprehensive about people who pushed Jewish practices upon others. Ignatius thought that anyone who put too much emphasis on Jewish law hadn't received the grace of God.

"But Ignatius was even more concerned about people teaching doctrines about Jesus that were not worthy of the character of Jesus. In Ignatius's day—and today as well, as you know—it is common for people who view spiritual things as good to also view physical things, such as our bodies, as evil. Ignatius was worried about ideas like these infiltrating our churches. So he affirmed that Jesus was himself God, but also insisted that Jesus as God had come in the flesh, physically suffered and died for our sins, and rose from the dead in his body. The idea that Jesus only appeared to be crucified, rather than actually and really being crucified, was viewed by Ignatius as a destructive and dangerous teaching; he would have called it a 'heresy.'"

"We're still wrestling with that one today," commented Rufina. "The knowing-ones are sympathetic with that idea, though their teachings go far beyond that."

Polycarp continued, "Ignatius tried to persuade those who would read his letters that the way to protect themselves doctrinally and ethically was to obey their bishop. But unlike the approach Clement took in his argument, Ignatius did not appeal to a line of succession from the apostles to the bishops. Instead, Ignatius assumed that the marks of the appointment from God should be self-evident in the bishop's godly demeanor, in the way he shares the mind of Christ, and in his truthful doctrinal affirmations about Jesus."

"So what happened after the squad and their prisoners left Troas?" asked Tavia.

"The ship docked in Neapolis," Polycarp replied, "and the party headed up the road toward Philippi. Ignatius, along with two other condemned Christians, Zosimus and Rufus, received encouragement and supplies from the Christians in Philippi, and then the band headed toward Rome . . . toward Ignatius's martyrdom. My big brother in the faith has been a model for me ever since he passed through Smyrna. I treasure the memory of my conversations with him and the letter he wrote just for me. I pray that I will stay faithful to death like Ignatius did."

The other four nodded their heads in solemn agreement. They were apprehensive, though, about what lay ahead for their beloved bishop.

Excerpts from the Letters of Ignatius

We welcomed in the Lord your well-loved name, which is yours through your righteous nature according to faith in and love of Christ Jesus our savior. As imitators of God, ignited by the blood of God, you perfectly completed the work that is so natural for you. For you made every effort to see me when you heard I was on my way from Syria in chains for our common name and hope. I am hoping through your prayers to succeed in fighting with wild beasts in Rome and thereby to be a disciple. (To the Ephesians 1.1–2)

Flee from divisions as the beginning of evils. You all must follow the bishop as Jesus Christ followed the Father, the council of elders as you would the apostles, and respect the deacons as you would God's command. Nobody should do anything having to do with the church without the bishop. Only regard as valid the Lord's Supper that is under the bishop, or whomever he designates. Wherever the bishop appears, there let the congregation be; just as wherever Christ Jesus is, there is the true church. It is not permitted to baptize or hold a love feast without the bishop, but whatever he approves pleases God. In this way whatever you do will be secure and valid. (To the Smyrnaeans 8.1–2)

So I exhort you—not I, but the love of Jesus Christ—only use Christian food. Stay away from every exotic plant, which is heresy. For these people deceitfully mix Jesus Christ with themselves. It is as if they were administering a deadly poison in honeyed wine, which the unsuspecting victim receives with delight and without fear, leading to a terrible death. (To the Trallians 6.1–2)

I am writing to all the churches and insisting to all that I am dying willingly for God—unless you hinder me. I beg you, do not try to be kind to me at the wrong moment. Let me be food for the wild beasts, for that is how I can get to God. I am God's wheat, and I am ground by the teeth of wild beasts that I may prove to be pure bread. I would prefer that you coax the wild beasts, that they can become my tomb and leave no scrap of my body, and that I might not be a burden to anyone after I die. Then when the world no longer sees my body I will truly be a disciple of Jesus Christ. Pray to God for me that through all these things I might prove to be God's sacrifice. I do not give orders like Peter and Paul. They were apostles; I am a convict. They were free; I am still a slave. But if I suffer, I shall become a freedman of Jesus Christ and rise up in him free. But now as a prisoner I am learning to desire nothing. (To the Romans 4.1–3)

Chapter 4

Polycarp's Letter to the Philippians
Tuesday Evening

"The stuffed grape leaves are outstanding—like my mother used to make. You're a wonderful cook, Tavia." Polycarp loosened his sash. "Might I bother you for one or two more?"

"With pleasure," replied Tavia. The deaconess scooped three of the tubular wraps onto Polycarp's plate, much to the elderly man's delight. She asked, "Polycarp, what happened to Ignatius after the company of soldiers left Macedonia? Did he send any more letters?"

"Not as far as I know," replied Polycarp. "The last letters anyone in our region received were the ones Bourrus brought from Troas. We did receive an update from a believing scribe named Crescens and his sister who came down to Smyrna from Philippi a few weeks later. They told us that the Philippian church had welcomed Ignatius and the other Christians when they passed through their city and had offered food and prayers for the trip ahead. But neither he nor his sister had any more information about Ignatius, and many months passed before we learned anything definite about his fate."

"Why were the two of them in Smyrna?" asked Tavia.

"Crescens and his sister were in Smyrna because they had been sent from the church in Philippi with a request."

"What request?"

"They wanted to ask me to arrange for their church to receive copies of the letters that Ignatius had written to the congregations in our region. Maybe they were feeling left out since they hadn't received a letter from Ignatius. So while we were waiting for news about Ignatius, Crescens and Bourrus started pulling together a collection of Ignatius's letters from the churches in the province. That process turned out to be useful in more than one way."

"Indeed," Bourrus added his agreement "gathering together those letters reminded us of how important it was for churches to maintain personal collections of Christian writings in their midst. For example, we already had benefited from a collection of the letters of the Apostle Paul we kept in Smyrna."

Polycarp concurred, "More and more collections of Christian writings were being brought together in various places. For this particular collection, I dictated a short letter that Crescens copied onto the beginning of a roll, then Crescens copied the letters of Ignatius onto the rest of the roll. When he was done, the scribe and his sister bid us farewell and headed north carrying their precious manuscript back to Philippi. At the time we still had not received any news from Rome about Ignatius's fate."

Artemidorus asked, "Did the church in Philippi appreciate what you had done?"

"Yes they did," answered Polycarp. "In fact, sometime later the church in Philippi sent another request."

"What request?"

"They wanted me to write them a real letter; not just a cover letter to go along with Ignatius's letters; they wanted a proper Christian letter written to their church about righteousness."

"Didn't you feel like they were imposing on you and your precious time?" asked Artemidorus. "Their church was among the early apostolic churches; it was founded by Paul himself. Not only that, but they received their own special letter from Paul—a joyful friendship letter. That's the letter you were quoting during our meeting in Smyrna this past Sunday, wasn't it?"

Polycarp nodded.

"Then they asked you to write them a letter about righteousness? In Smyrna we never received such a letter—except for the little letter in John's apocalypse . . . oh, and the letter from Ignatius. . . . But Smyrna is a far more prominent city than little Philippi . . . and they already have a letter from an apostle. Why should they get one from Polycarp?"

Polycarp spoke softly, "I was glad to respond to their request. You need to realize that the church in Philippi was facing some difficult times. You might have been more sympathetic if you'd been alive at the time and had known what troubles the church was facing."

"What was going on?" inquired Rufina.

"The church in Philippi was under pressure both from the outside and from the inside. The decision by the Philippian Christians to acknowledge Ignatius and other Christian prisoners was not well-received by locals. Showing sympathy and extending help to convicts in transit to Rome to face execution, especially by strangers where the only connection to the criminal is a shared philosophical viewpoint, is not popular, especially in a city housing so many retired Roman soldiers. In my letter I exhorted the Philippian Christians to patiently endure their sufferings and follow the examples of those who had suffered before them, including Ignatius, Zosimus, and Rufus, as well as others from their own congregation—not to mention the apostles and their founder Paul. But since all of these had followed Christ in suffering, I wanted to remind the Christians in Philippi also to be imitators of their Lord when they suffered.

"But the most difficult thing the congregation was facing wasn't external pressure. In my opinion the internal trials were more risky to the congregation than any external persecution they might have experienced. The biggest problem was Valens . . . and his wife."

"Valens?" questioned Rufina.

"Valens was a former elder of the Philippian church. I didn't mention him directly until later in my letter, but I planned to write about his situation from the time I started dictating it. I prepared the Philippian readers for what I would later say about Valens by warning at a few points in the letter against the love of money. You see, Valens's greed had overtaken him to such a degree that he lost track of the integrity required for one who had been given such an honorable place of leadership by God. He hid things—with full knowledge of his wife—and began to tell untruths about what he had done with the church's money. He didn't exercise self-control, even though he was preaching self-control to others. When his deeds came out into the light, it became clear that he couldn't continue in his role as a church overseer. But because of his relationships with so many in the congregation, he kept in contact with some of them—still viewing himself as a Christian—even though he and his wife were unwilling to publicly repent of what they had done. I was mortified at the thought that an elder of one of the earliest churches would do such a thing, and afraid that his greedy idolatry might eventually split the congregation."

"So you told them to cut off Valens and his wife, right?" interrupted Artemidorus.

"No, I counseled the acting elders to be measured in their approach—not to treat the couple as enemies of the church, but rather as sick and straying members."

"But if you really thought that their actions posed a greater risk to the congregation than outward persecution . . . " averred Artemidorus, "don't you think that stronger action was necessary?"

"A doctor tries medicine on an infection before he cuts off a limb."

"Yes, but another proverb reminds us that someone who burns his tongue while drinking hot milk will instinctively blow even on cold yogurt."

Polycarp looked up with affection at his young—but often impetuous—assistant. "Artemidorus, patience is often advised in instances like this. I was hoping that in Valens's case the hot milk might have cooled just enough that he wouldn't burn the congregation during the period they were trying to lead him back to repentance."

"But . . . "

Rufina intervened, "Perhaps we should hear more about the letter? What did you mean when you said that the Philippians had asked you to write about righteousness? What did they mean by righteousness?"

"They wanted me to give practical advice about how to live a righteous life. But since righteousness relates both to belief and to behavior—right beliefs produce right behavior whereas wrong beliefs produce wrong behavior—I started my letter emphasizing what we believe. Our faith is based upon our Lord Jesus Christ, who endured death for our sins, and whom God raised from the dead. As Paul wrote, we have received salvation by grace, not by works. Salvation is by the will of God through Jesus Christ.

"But it doesn't stop there; such truth only lays the foundation for lives filled with righteous living. I wrote to the Philippians that they needed to leave behind the emptiness and error of the crowd and demonstrate their belief in the one who raised Jesus from the dead by following his will, keeping his commandments, and loving the things he loved. I warned them to avoid unrighteousness, slander, and false testimony—and, of course, the love of money. I counseled them to remember what the Lord taught: 'Do not judge, so that you may not be judged; forgive, and you will be forgiven; show mercy, so that you may be shown mercy,' and 'blessed are the poor and those who are persecuted for the sake of righteousness, for theirs is the kingdom of God.' Furthermore, since they were facing societal pressures from the world—along with all churches then and now—I encouraged them to maintain a good standard of conduct among unbelievers, to avoid temptation, to bear up under persecution, and to pray for kings and others in authority.

"The Apostle Paul was the founder of their church, and since they already had a letter written by him, I tried to persuade them to righteous living by making connections with Paul. I filled my letter with allusions to lots of earlier writings, but especially to things Paul had written, whom I mentioned by name at three different points in the letter. I tried to write in a style similar to Paul's letters and kept encouraging them to imitate the example of their blessed and glorious apostle."

"Did you offer any doctrinal warnings?" asked Tavia.

"Yes, since we in Smyrna were constantly encountering professing Christians who denied that Jesus Christ had a fully human body—the same people Ignatius had warned about—I added my own warning to that effect. I quoted from the letter of the Apostle John who stated that anyone who denied Jesus' fleshly body was an antichrist and that anyone who denied the testimony of the cross was of the devil.

"But the majority of the letter was an attempt to encourage the Philippian Christians to live out the righteous lives God had called them to live. I encouraged wives to cherish their husbands and teach their children the way of the Lord. I reminded widows that they are God's altar, and so need to keep their thoughts and intentions pure as they offer sacrifices of prayer. I called on deacons to serve others the way the Lord served. I warned young men to be sexually pure and to obey the elders and deacons, and young women to uphold a pure and blameless conscience.

"I also addressed the elders in Philippi and sought to prod them toward acts of compassion and mercy while they safeguarded righteous character. But as I was writing the instructions to the elders, I switched mid-stream and started using the word 'we,' since I was reminding myself of these instructions, being an elder myself."

"You mean bishop, right?" asked Artemidorus.

"No, as I explained before, this was a period of transition. I was a leading elder, but I was still an elder—and the word bishop still meant pretty much the same thing as elder in those days. If you get a chance to read the letter, you will notice that my first words are: 'Polycarp and the elders with him.' Ignatius's encouragement did help move our churches toward centralizing leadership around a bishop, toward the kind of authority I exercise now. But that transition was not complete when I wrote the letter to the Philippians."

"What happened to the letter after you finished it?" prodded Tavia.

Polycarp nodded to Bourrus, who explained, "After Polycarp dictated the letter we wrapped it carefully and sent it off with someone who was traveling toward Philippi. The letter was well–received by the Philippians. They treasured it, and eventually made copies for other churches. But they decided to combine this letter about righteousness—which was actually Polycarp's second letter to the Philippians—with the first letter, the little cover letter he had sent along with the Ignatian letters. So both letters are joined together in one document in most of the copies found today."

"All I can say," remarked Artemidorus, "is that the Philippians were lucky to even get a letter from someone as important as you."

"I was glad to write it for them," replied Polycarp meekly. "I'm grateful to be able to serve the church of God in any way I can."

Excerpts from Polycarp's Letter to the Philippians

Polycarp and the elders with him, to the church of God that sojourns at Philippi. May mercy and peace be multiplied to you from God Almighty and Jesus Christ our Savior. I greatly rejoice with you in our Lord Jesus Christ because you did the right thing in welcoming the models of true love. You helped on their way those bound in holy chains, which are the crowns of the ones truly chosen by God and our Lord. I also rejoice because the firm root of your faith, announced from early times, still remains and continues to bear fruit for our Lord Jesus Christ, who endured for our sins to the point of death, and whom God raised up, having loosed the birth–pains of Hades. Even though you have not seen him you believe in him with an inexpressible and glorious joy that many long to experience. For you know that by grace you have been saved, not by works, but by the will of God through Jesus Christ. (Salutation—1.3)

I am not writing these things about righteousness, brothers and sisters, on my own initiative, but because you invited me. For neither I nor anyone like me can match the wisdom of the blessed and glorious Paul. When he was with you in the presence of the people of that time, he carefully and reliably taught you the word of truth; when he was absent he wrote you letters. If you examine them you will

be able to build yourselves up in the faith given to you.
(3.1–2)

For whoever does not confess that Jesus Christ has come in
the flesh is an antichrist. And whoever does not confess the
testimony of the cross is of the devil. And whoever distorts
the sayings of the Lord for his own desires and claims that
there is neither resurrection nor judgment, this one is the
firstborn of Satan. Therefore we must abandon the futility
of the crowd and their false teachings and return to the
word given to us from the beginning. Let us be attentive
to prayer and devoted to fasting, fervently requesting the
all–seeing God not to lead us into temptation. As the Lord
said, "The spirit is willing, but the flesh is weak." (7.1–2)

I am deeply grieved for Valens, who once was an elder
among you, because he so forgets the position that was given
to him. I warn you, therefore, avoid love of money, and be
pure and truthful. Avoid every form of evil. But how can
someone who cannot control himself in these things teach
another? If anyone does not avoid the love of money he will
be defiled by idolatry and will be judged as if he were one
of the Gentiles who do not know the judgment of the Lord.
(11.1–2)

Chapter 5

The Didache

Wednesday Morning

"CROCUS, YOU'RE HERE!" POLYCARP stood up as straight as he was able and greeted his great-nephew with a hug. "I'm so happy to see you! But what's the matter? Are you upset?"

"The authorities are still looking for you and asking lots of uncomfortable questions. Their questions are increasingly accompanied by threats. Uncle Polycarp, I'm not sure that hiding is a good idea. You're putting your family in an awkward position—not to mention those you refer to as your spiritual family."

"Oh, Crocus, I am so very sorry about all this. I don't want my Christian faith to put anyone at risk, especially those I love. Perhaps if I came back to Smyrna, I could speak to the authorities . . . "

"And then what?" interrupted Artemidorus. "Try to convince them that you're a nice old man and that they should leave you and all the rest of us alone?"

Polycarp replied, "But I am a nice old man! Maybe if I took along a generous plate of Tavia's stuffed grape leaves for Herod—our nice chief constable—he might take a liking to me!"

Crocus looked uncomfortable, "I really don't think this is the time for humor, Uncle."

"Then what should I do, Crocus? Be honest with me."

"I could take you back to Smyrna. It might just work for you to talk to the security chief. You could explain to him that you and your Christian friends have never been a danger to the peace of the city. He'll respect your age. He'll respond to your dignity. Uncle, I know that you show respect to the governing authorities. I've heard you say so and I've seen it in your actions."

"Yes, I have said that, and I've tried to live it out as well."

"I think I've even heard you tell others to pray for governmental leaders."

"Yes, I've said that too."

"So, explain all that to the constable. Tell him that you have always been submissive to the government, never incited rebellion, and always paid your taxes. Such a conversation could take the pressure off your friends and family members."

Polycarp was pensive, but did not respond. Bourrus turned and spoke to the young man gently, but directly, "Have you so quickly forgotten what happened to Germanicus?"

"Oh yes . . . Germanicus . . . that was horrible. But—please forgive me for what I'm going to say—Germanicus brought it upon himself. In his zeal he acted like he *wanted* to die. If he hadn't been so stubborn, he could have . . . "

"He could have what?!" demanded Artemidorus.

"He could have done what the proconsul offered him."

"Swear to the genius of Caesar and offer the sacrifice? Really, Crocus? You have known Christians all your life. Don't you realize that our highest allegiance is to Christ, to Jesus our king?" Artemidorus was agitated.

"That's the kind of talk that gets Christians in trouble. That's the stubbornness . . . "

Polycarp intervened. "Crocus, Jesus is my king, and in one respect, yours too. But you need to acknowledge it. For now I must stay here, since that is what the believers in Smyrna have asked me to do. I honor them best by respecting their request."

"Unfortunately, that's exactly what I thought you'd say, Uncle. I wish you would reconsider."

Polycarp gazed intently at him, "There are only two ways, my dear nephew, one of life and one of death, and there is a great difference between these two ways. The one who walks in the way of life loves the God who created him and loves his neighbor as himself. My nephew, how long will you wait to start walking the way of life?"

Crocus looked uncomfortable, eyed everyone in the group, and finally spoke, "It's time for me to leave. I have business to attend to in Smyrna."

Rufina moved quickly and placed her hand on his shoulder, "Please, Crocus, don't feel you have to leave. We're happy for you to stay longer. You are welcome with us."

"No, I really need to go." And with that he gathered his things and was gone.

When the group of five was alone, Rufina was the first to speak, "Poor Crocus. All these years . . . and he still doesn't understand."

"Poor Crocus?" snapped Artemidorus. "He knows full well—and yet refuses to believe. It's like he's choosing the way of death over the way of life, like Polycarp talked about."

Tavia decided it was time to change the subject. "Where was that expression from, anyway, Polycarp? What were you quoting when you used that expression a minute ago?"

"Which expression?"

"The way of life and the way of death."

"Jews and Christians have been picturing the way of life in contrast to the way of death for as long as I can remember. The idea is found in the blessings and curses section of the old covenant writings, and Jesus himself contrasted the wide gate and way that leads to destruction with the narrow gate and way that leads to life. But when I mentioned it just now, I was quoting from the first line of a document I learned about when Ignatius came through Smyrna on his journey toward Rome."

"A document from Antioch in Syria?"

"Yes. When I asked Ignatius how the church in Antioch was organized, he mentioned that their church sometimes consulted a roll containing some teachings of the Lord through the apostles as well as practical instructions for church life. He explained that the document had started as a small collection of ethical instructions for new converts, but had later been combined with other practical guidelines for how to run local churches. The ethical section in combination with the practical church advice section—plus a bit of writing about the end of the age—has been circulating together for quite a while now, helping churches both in Syria and beyond."

"Are they actually teachings of the Lord through the apostles?" asked Tavia.

"Some of them are, especially in the first half of the document, in the section that describes the way of life and the way of death. We know some are genuine sayings of the Lord because in certain cases they agree with other trustworthy streams of tradition. But there are other teachings in this manuscript, both in the ethical section and in the practical church life section, that arose out of the needs of the churches in Syria. Those instructions were not originally spoken by Jesus, but by faithful Christians."

"What are some of the genuine teachings of Jesus in this writing?" asked Rufina.

"Pray for your enemies, turn the other cheek to the one who strikes you, go two miles instead of one, give away your tunic to the person who asks for your cloak."

"I'm familiar with all of those."

"But the text also includes other warnings to avoid evil, especially the types of practices that would have been offensive to Jewish Christians."

"Such as?"

"Well-known commands from the law of Moses like not murdering, committing adultery, stealing, coveting, or bearing false testimony . . . but also the avoidance of magic and sorcery, and the refusal to abort children or commit infanticide."

"As I remember," Bourrus interposed, "the first section—the part that is full of ethical instruction for new believers—was originally pulled together for Christians of Jewish descent. Am I correct about that?"

"Yes, that's what it looks like to me. All Christians from Jewish backgrounds have struggled to understand the role of the old covenant law in their Christian lives. The advice this writing offers to those struggling with what to do with the law is: 'If you can bear the whole yoke of the Lord, you will be perfect. But if you cannot, then do what you are able.'"

"And the yoke is a metaphor for the law . . . " said Bourrus.

"That's right."

"But what about the rest of the document?" pursued Tavia. "What is it about?"

"The largest part of this writing is practical advice for managing common church issues."

"Like what?"

"First, there are instructions about baptism. Baptism is to be in the name of the Father, the Son, and the Holy Spirit. Baptism is best carried out in cold running water, though it is acceptable to baptize in warm water if cold isn't available. If neither of these is possible, then you can pour water on the initiate's head three times . . ."

"In the name of the Father, the Son, and the Holy Spirit." Artemidorus finished the sentence.

"Correct. Fasting is recommended for one or two days before baptism, both for the one being baptized and the one baptizing, as well as for any other believers who can join in the fast."

"Is there anything more about fasting?" asked Rufina, who had found fasting to be spiritually helpful to her.

"Fasting should take place two days a week, on Wednesdays and Fridays."

"Wednesdays and Fridays?" asked Artemidorus. "Why those days?"

"It's not that those days are special, but they contrast with the Jewish practice of fasting on Mondays and Thursdays, and our practice should be different from what the Jews practice. The way we pray should also contrast with Jewish prayers. For example, three times a day you should pray the Lord 's Prayer.

"There are also instructions for the celebration of the Lord's Supper. The only people who should eat and drink the Lord's Supper are those who have been baptized. One particular prayer is recommended for everyone to say during this meal of thanks, and another for when the meal is finished. But the prophets can offer thanks any way they want."

"Prophets and prophecy . . . " Bourrus sighed. "Now that's an issue that hasn't always been easy in our ministry in Smyrna."

"No, it hasn't, though we must be careful, as Paul reminded us, not to despise prophetic utterances. Actually, one of the sections of this document that has been most helpful to me in my ministry has been the instructions for how to handle Christian visitors who claim to be prophets, apostles, or teachers. Some valuable recommendations are given in this document."

"Such as?" probed Tavia.

"Such as . . . let me ask you. How can you recognize that a false prophet is in fact false?"

"If he teaches something that is contrary to the doctrine we have received?" suggested Tavia.

"Yes, that's right. But also if a prophet stays more than two days in one house, he is false. If he asks for money—especially if he asks for it while he's supposedly in the Spirit—you'll know he's taking advantage of you. Also, if he doesn't exhibit the Lord's ways in his conduct, or personally doesn't practice what he prophesies, he is false."

"What about others who aren't prophets who pass through town? Is there any guidance for how to handle them?" asked Tavia.

"Travelers who come in the name of the Lord should be welcomed, fed, and helped on their way by Christians. But as with the advice given about prophets, such people shouldn't stay more than two days—or three if absolutely necessary—unless their intentions are to remain long-term with you. If a person wants to settle down and knows a trade, he should start working. Otherwise, the church needs to figure out a way for him to live in their midst without being idle. If he's new to the congregation, but won't accept the church's decision in this matter, you'll know he's taking advantage of your hospitality."

"That works fine for a regular Christian, but what if the person who wants to stay is a prophet or teacher?" asked Rufina.

"If any prophets or teachers settle among you, the church should support them with the first fruits of money and goods that have been set aside for such a purpose. If you have no teachers or prophets in your midst, then the money you have collected for this cause can be used to help the poor."

"Only prophets and teachers should be supported?" asked Tavia.

"No. Bishops—which in that writing meant the same thing as elders means to us today—and deacons can also be supported."

"Are bishops and deacons actually mentioned in the document?"

"Yes, bishops and deacons are to be appointed who are humble, who don't love money, and who have been tested and approved. They are to be honored alongside prophets and teachers. Today we place greater emphasis on bishops, elders, and deacons than we do on prophets, but in those days, prophets were honored alongside regular leaders."

"That advice is all very helpful. I need to pull out this document and look at it again soon," said Bourrus. "I've forgotten, though, how it ends."

"The document finishes with a list of Jesus' warnings about the times just before his glorious return. False prophets will arise, the sheep will turn into wolves, and love will turn into hate. Persecution will keep increasing until the deceiver of the world appears as a son of God, performing signs and wonders—abominations they are called. In those days, many will fall away, but those who endure will be saved. Finally, the world will see the Lord coming upon the clouds of heaven . . . "

"Come quickly, Lord Jesus," Rufina spontaneous prayed.

The other four responded in kind: "Yes, come quickly."

Excerpts from The Didache

There are two ways, one of life and one of death. There is a great difference between the two ways. Now this is the way of life: first, you shall love the God who made you; second, you shall love your neighbor as yourself. Whatever you do not want done to you, do not do to someone else. (1.1–2)

The second commandment of the teaching is: Do not murder. Do not commit adultery. Do not corrupt children. Do not be sexually immoral. Do not steal. Do not practice magic. Do not murder a child by abortion, nor kill it at birth. Do not covet your neighbor's possessions. (2.1)

The way of death is this: first of all it is evil and full of cursing—murders, adulteries, lusts, sexual immoralities, thefts, idolatries, magical practices, sorceries, robberies, false testimonies, hypocrisies, duplicities, deceit, self-importance, meanness, stubbornness, greed, foul language, jealousy, brashness, pride, arrogance. (5.1)

Now about baptism: this is how to baptize. After you have explained all these things ahead of time, baptize in running water in the name of the Father and of the Son and of the Holy Spirit. But if you do not have running water, baptize in something else. If you cannot baptize in cold water, then do it in warm. If you have neither, pour water on the head three times in the name of the Father and the Son and the Holy Spirit. (7.1–3)

Your fasts should not be like the hypocrites. They fast on Monday and Thursday, but you should fast on Wednesday and Friday. Nor should you pray like the hypocrites. Instead pray like the Lord commanded in his gospel: "Our father in heaven . . . " (8.1–2)

Now about apostles and prophets, act in accord with the rule of the gospel. Every apostle who comes to you should be welcomed as you would welcome the Lord. But he should not stay more than one day, unless there is a need, in which case he can stay one more day. But if he stays three, he is a false prophet. When the apostle leaves he must not take anything except bread to get him to his next night's stay. If he asks for money, he is a false prophet. (11.3–6)

Chapter 6

Papias

Wednesday Evening

"WHAT'S THE MATTER, TAVIA?" Rufina placed her hand on the younger woman's shoulder. "Is something troubling you?"

"It's probably nothing," Tavia responded. "It's just that . . . I saw Crocus talking with a neighbor when I was disposing some garbage this morning after breakfast."

"With a neighbor?" Artemidorus walked into their conversation. "What was Crocus doing talking to a neighbor while we're hiding out here?"

"I don't know; that's why I'm mentioning it. I'm pretty sure he didn't see me; he was at a distance and there were a few trees between us. But their conversation appeared animated."

"I don't like it at all," said Artemidorus.

"You don't like what?" asked Bourrus, who had just walked over. Now everyone was in the conversation, including Polycarp, who had just entered the courtyard.

"Crocus was talking to a neighbor," Artemidorus responded. "Tavia saw him."

"I'm sure there is a reasonable explanation," piped in Polycarp as he nonchalantly took a seat for breakfast. "Come and sit with me. Now, what's this about Crocus, Tavia?"

"Shortly after we finished breakfast I saw him talking to a woman in the first farm house down the road."

"Didn't he say that he needed to hurry back to Smyrna?" asked Polycarp.

"He did. So what was he doing talking to someone out here?"

Polycarp replied, "It really could have been anything, Tavia. Think about it. Maybe he ran into someone he knew. Or maybe the woman needed his help in some way. He's been known to stop and help people in need."

"You're right, of course. But it still surprised me; particularly since we're doing everything we can to keep your presence here a secret."

"Crocus is a respectable young man," said Rufina. "I've watched him grow up. I'm terribly sad that he continues to reject our Lord. But he still maintains many good and close relationships with Christians, including with his great uncle Polycarp."

"I don't like it," said Artemidorus a second time. "What if the neighbors discover that Polycarp is here?"

Polycarp intercepted the conversation, "There really isn't anything to do about it, is there? And worrying never added a single hour to a person's life. I learned that lesson a long time ago. It's a good thing, too, considering I've spent most of my adult life trying to lead a church; and that allows for plenty of things to worry about! Maybe this would be a good time to dive into our topic for the evening. What would you like to discuss?"

Bourrus gladly took the lead: "A couple of us were thinking that it might be helpful if we could talk a bit about bishop Papias. He was an interesting character. I heard him give a message at a house church meeting a long time ago in Smyrna."

"I forgot that you ever had contact with Papias," said Polycarp.

"You knew him fairly well, didn't you?" asked Bourrus.

"I saw him occasionally over the years. His town of Hierapolis is still within our province, but is far enough away from Smyrna that I only got out there a few times during my lifetime. I saw him most frequently during my younger years when a visit of his to Ephesus would overlap with one of my own. As he got older and took on greater amounts of church responsibility in Hierapolis, he still occasionally made the trek out to Ephesus or Smyrna. It must have been on one of those trips that you heard him speak."

"What was he like?" asked Rufina.

"He was bookish," replied Polycarp. "He didn't appreciate people who talked a lot. He was interested in the past—very focused on history."

"He knew John too, didn't he?"

"Yes, and that's primarily how I got to know him early on, since I'd get down to Ephesus to have conversations with John whenever I could. Papias was obsessed about talking to people who carried around in their memories the teachings of Jesus and the apostles. So in his younger years he came out to the coast as often as he could to talk to John and another disciple named Aristion, since from them he could listen to what he called 'a living and continuing voice,' that is, the living and continuing voice of the Lord. Those were the times I first got to know him."

"But he already had access to a deep stream of tradition in his own town of Hierapolis, didn't he, Polycarp?" asked Bourrus.

"Yes indeed, and 'stream' is a good metaphor, especially for Hierapolis. The water flowing out of the mountain is full of minerals that harden into white cascading pools. The mineral deposits produce a natural formation on the hills just below Hierapolis unlike anything else I've ever seen. When you view it from a distance, say from Laodicea, it looks like snow, even in the summer, but as you approach the formation. . . . "

"Wasn't the water supposed to be a metaphor for traditions passed on orally?" interjected Artemidorus.

"Oh, yes . . . it was a metaphor. . . . But Hierapolis is really interesting! So, the stream of tradition I was referring to was the daughters of Philip. Philip's daughters had taken up residence in Hierapolis with their father after the Jewish wars. Since Philip's daughters lived to be quite old, they functioned for Papias like a constant flowing stream filled with sayings of Jesus and apostolic traditions. Papias was able to draw upon them to build up a deposit of traditions right where he was living that linked him to the apostolic age. Besides talking with those godly women, Papias took as many opportunities as he could to interview people from the first generation and those who had come in contact with disciples of Jesus. He wrote down what he heard, added those traditions to what he had learned from John, Aristion, and the daughters of Philip, then organized them into logical groupings, and so laid down a deposit of written traditions for the next generation."

"What was the name of his volume again, Polycarp?" asked Tavia.

"*Expositions of the Sayings of the Lord.* His collection actually fills five large volumes. It's a good thing that Christians are increasingly employing the codex form instead of the more traditional rolls for our copies of books these days. Otherwise, because of the size of Papias's life work, it would be difficult to locate anything in it. Papias's goal was to organize sayings of the Lord into logical groupings and make occasional comments about them along the way."

"Why write down sayings of Jesus if there were already written gospels around? Didn't Papias know about them?" asked Artemidorus.

"Yes, of course he did. But Papias valued oral tradition over written documents. In his opinion, written information wasn't as useful as information from a living and continuing voice."

"That's a bit ironic, considering that he wrote down what he heard, isn't it?" commented Tavia. "And did he say anything about written gospels? Did he mention any in particular?"

"He commented on the composition of the gospel of Mark. He said that Mark was Peter's interpreter and that Mark accurately wrote down whatever he heard from Peter about Jesus' life and teaching. Papias seemed to think that Mark could have ordered his account better—maybe more like his own organizational structure!—but still believed that Mark had been careful to include nothing inaccurate in what he wrote."

"I like the structure of Mark's gospel; I'm not sure what Papias's problem with it was," commented Bourrus. "Mark's gospel actively moves a reader along and then reverently focuses everyone's attention on the death of Jesus."

"I like it too," added his wife.

Polycarp continued, "Papias also mentioned the gospel of Matthew, which he thought was ordered better than Mark's. He said that Matthew composed his oracles in the Hebrew language. Some have taken this to mean that Matthew originally wrote his gospel in the language of Palestine, and then translated it into Greek. But the only gospel associated with Matthew we've ever seen in Smyrna is a Greek document, and it isn't translational Greek. I don't think Papias ever actually saw a Hebrew manuscript; he was just passing on something he had heard from one of his interviews."

"Did Papias record anything that isn't found in the gospels most familiar to us in Smyrna?"

"Yes he did, as a matter of fact. Papias relates a saying of Jesus to Judas that isn't in other written gospels. One day Judas, in his unbelief, asked Jesus whether such incredible growth as Jesus was predicting could really happen. Jesus is said to reply, 'Those who live until those times will see.'"

"That's a saying I've never heard before," commented Tavia. "Did he mention any other less–familiar traditions?"

"You may remember that when the apostles cast lots to decide which of two men should replace Judas, Matthias was the one who was chosen. But Papias wrote down a tradition about the man who wasn't chosen, Joseph, whom most knew as Barsabbas. When Barsabbas was put to the test by unbelievers, he drank snake poison in the name of Christ and was protected from harm. This was one of many such accounts Papias heard from the daughters of Philip."

Bourrus commented, "What were his views about the future? If my memory serves me, the one time I heard Papias speak in Smyrna, he was trying to defend his view of what would happen after the resurrection of the faithful. I believe that there was some discussion with Papias about what he said that day—friendly disagreement you might say—by those who heard what he presented, including, if I'm not mistaken, by you Polycarp!"

Polycarp laughed, "Yes, Papias and I disagreed about some details of how the future will unfold, though," the bishop was quick to add, "we agreed on everything essential. We agreed that God will raise us up from the dead as he promised and that we will also reign with him. What is more essential than that?"

"So what do you disagree about?" asked Artemidorus.

"Hasten not to enter controversies, my young friend," cautioned Polycarp, "unless such controversies are essential for maintaining the faith once delivered. Our disagreement was not about basic Christian belief. Papias and I disagreed on whether there will be a literal millennium at the end of the age."

"Millennium?" asked Artemidorus. "A thousand years of what?"

"Of peace and prosperity," replied Polycarp. "Actually, we both agreed that the apostles referred to a millennium. Our disagreement was about whether we should interpret such references literally, as Papias alleged, or figuratively, as I thought and continue to think."

"What did he think the millennium would be like?" asked Artemidorus.

"He imagined a place of abundant food springing up from a fertile and productive soil watered from the dew of heaven. Animals who fed on the food grown in this special soil would turn tranquil and live in peace with each other under the leadership of humans. Every vine would produce ten thousand shoots, each shoot would produce ten thousand branches, from each branch would sprout ten thousand twigs, from each twig would hang ten thousand clusters, and from each cluster ten thousand grapes! The more I thought about such a vineyard, the harder it became to imagine trying to walk through it!"

Artemidorus laughed as he tried to imagine it. "But such big numbers sound figurative to me, rather than literal."

"No, my young assistant, Papias would have viewed them as intended exaggeration that pointed toward the abundance of a literal reality, a tangible millennium that would spring up after the resurrection of the saints. The millennium for Papias was real, something that would actually take place on earth at the end of the age. Christians continue to disagree on this question."

"Well, I'm always up for good food . . . and lots of it!" exclaimed Artemidorus.

"Don't I know it!" replied Tavia. "I had no idea how much food I was going to need to feed you! You eat almost as much as everyone else together!"

To this comment Artemidorus had no reply. But the thought of eating bowls and bowls of luscious grapes made him hope that Papias might be right after all.

Excerpts from the Fragments of Papias

I will not hesitate to present to you everything I carefully learned from the elders and carefully retained in my memory, along with my interpretations, and insist that they are true. For unlike most people I did not appreciate those who have lots to say, but those who teach the truth. Nor did I appreciate those who remember the commands of others, but rather those who remember the commands given by the Lord for the faith that comes from the truth itself. And if by chance someone should pass through who had actually been a follower of the elders, I questioned them about the words of the elders: what Andrew or what Peter, or what Thomas or James, or what John or Matthew, or some other of the Lord's disciples said—and whatever the Lord's disciples Aristion and the elder John were saying. For I assumed that what comes from books is not as useful to me as what comes from a living and continuing voice. (Papias in Eusebius, Church History 3.39)

Mark, since he was Peter's interpreter, accurately, but not in order, wrote down all he remembered of the things that were either said or done by Christ. For he neither heard the Lord nor followed him, but later, as I said, followed Peter. He presented the teachings as needed, but not as an organized account of the sayings of the Lord. So Mark did nothing wrong when he wrote down some of them as he remembered them, for he was concerned about one thing, not to omit anything that he heard nor to include anything false in them. *(Papias in Eusebius, Church History 3.39)*

So Matthew gave an organized account of the sayings in the Hebrew language, and each person interpreted them as he was able. *(Papias in Eusebius, Church History 3.39)*

The days will come when vines will grow, each with ten thousand shoots, and on a single shoot ten thousand branches, and on a single branch ten thousand twigs, and on a single twig ten thousand clusters, and on a single cluster ten thousand grapes. And every grape when pressed will yield twenty-five measures of wine. When one of the saints grabs a cluster, another cluster will cry out:"I am better, take me, bless the Lord because of me." Similarly, a grain of wheat will yield ten thousand heads, and every head ten thousand grains, and every grain ten pounds of pure white flour. And the other fruits and seeds and grass will yield comparable amounts. All the animals that eat foods produced by the ground will live peacefully and harmoniously together, entirely subject to humans. (Papias in Irenaeus, Against Heresies 5.33.3–4)

Chapter 7

The Shepherd of Hermas

Thursday Morning

"ARE YOU SURE YOU weren't asleep?" asked Rufina, alarmed by what she had just heard. "Maybe it was a just a dream . . . frightening, I admit, but still a regular dream."

"No," insisted Polycarp, "It was not a dream. I was wide awake. God gave me a vision."

"Then please tell us again what happened, Polycarp, including any details," entreated Bourrus.

"I awoke early this morning, and spent a long time praying. It was a period of agonized prayer. I asked God to protect me from fear, and that I would stand as an example of faithfulness to our congregation. I prayed for the families of those who have recently lost loved ones in Smyrna, and I spoke to the Lord about each of the four of you by name. Then, suddenly, without any warning, my pillow burst into flames. I raised my arm to shield my eyes from the light and tried to get away from the fire because of its intense heat. I started to call out to you for help, when all of a sudden the fire went out . . . as quickly as it had started. It took a moment to grasp the significance of what had just occurred. I gingerly reached over and touched the pillow, but it was cool to the touch, and there was absolutely nothing that suggested that the pillow had been on fire. I realized in that moment that God had sent me a vision of what is to come."

"But what does it mean?" asked Tavia.

"Isn't it obvious?" Polycarp articulated the last words any of them wanted to hear. He spoke gently but directly. "It is necessary that I be burned alive."

"No!" cried Artemidorus. "Maybe the fire points to something else! Maybe God is going to give you a new zeal for prayer . . . or he is going to spread his truth throughout our city like a wildfire . . . or somehow passions for sin will be purified by fire in God's presence!"

"No, my friend, God sent a vision to prepare me—and all of you—for what is to come."

"But . . . I can't face that! You have been . . . a father to me. No, more than a father!" Tears streamed down the burly young man's face.

Polycarp placed both hands on Artemidorus's shoulders, looked at the others in the group and offered words of encouragement to them, "We need to hold tightly and without wavering to our hope. Our hope is Christ Jesus himself, who carried our sins in his body on the tree. He committed no sin, and no deceit was found in his mouth; instead he endured everything for our sake. We must seek to imitate his endurance, and if we have to suffer for the sake of his name, we must do it in a way that glorifies his name. This is the example he set for us."

After a long silence, Rufina spoke, "May the Lord's will be done."

Artemidorus looked up in shock, and was about to object, but Bourrus didn't give him an opportunity, instead recommending that they spend some time in prayer. Bourrus led out by praying himself. When everyone else—except Artemidorus—had prayed, Bourrus closed in the name of the Father, Son, and Holy Spirit. Then Bourrus said, "We cannot, and should not, spend the entire day talking about this vision, since there is little we can do, besides prayer, in response to it."

"I couldn't agree more!" seconded Polycarp. "Let's have some conversation about another Christian writing, shall we?"

"I'd like to talk about the revelations of Hermas," suggested Tavia. "Now there's someone who saw a lot of visions . . . "

"Hmm. . . . I'm willing to talk about this, but you should know in advance that I have reservations about some aspects of his writing," said Polycarp.

"But it's very popular among Christians," responded Tavia. "Is it the visions you are unsure about? Do you think Hermas didn't actually see them?"

"I would never deny that God gives visions to his people," Polycarp replied. "Obviously I believe in visions since I believe God just gave me one. I think that Hermas was a prophet who received numerous visions from God. His book has been an encouragement and challenge to many. But I wonder about some of the applications he makes from the visions he saw."

"But weren't a lot of his interpretations given to him by the shepherd?" asked Rufina. "How could the shepherd be wrong?"

Artemidorus jumped in, "Well, it sounds like all of you already know everything about this book, but I'm afraid I don't. Could someone at least tell me what we're talking about? And how could a shepherd's interpretation always be correct?"

Rufina laughed, "We're not talking about a regular shepherd, Artemidorus. The shepherd of Hermas was an angel that Hermas asserts was sent to guide him through his visions."

"So, who was Hermas?" asked Artemidorus, still confused.

"Hermas was a prophet who lived in Rome. His early ministry overlapped with the time of Clement," submitted Bourrus.

Rufina added, "It's interesting, though, that Hermas never in his writings referred to himself as a prophet, even though he wanted Christians to receive his revelations as true—in contrast to people he counted as false prophets."

"That's right; he doesn't refer to himself as a prophet directly," added Bourrus, "but people still regard Hermas as a prophet—and I think rightly so."

"When did he write?" asked Artemidorus.

"His writings didn't come together all at once," said Bourrus. "Hermas received various revelations and visions from God over the years. His book divides neatly into five visions, ten commandments, and twelve parables. But Hermas actually released his revelations in three stages—at least in their written form. The first stage included four visions along with their interpretations. At a later time Hermas pulled together ten sections of what he calls commandments, plus ten parables." Bourrus looked over at Artemidorus, "That's the section where the shepherd—the angel—shows up." Bourrus continued, "Sometime later, the visions were joined together with the commandments and the parables by adding one additional vision to the earlier four visions, and by adding two long parables to the end of the commandments/parables section in an attempt to somehow connect everything."

"You should know, though, that the reason people are drawn to this document isn't because of its logical flow," commented Rufina. "Hermas repeated ideas over and over, even though he utilized various images to present and develop those ideas."

"Then why is it so popular?" asked Artemidorus.

"Maybe it's because Hermas used regular language in his writing that connects with regular people," replied Rufina. "Or maybe it's because people have trouble containing their curiosity about new revelations."

"Bourrus, do you know if he was ever in leadership in the Roman church?" asked Tavia.

"No, he wasn't in leadership," answered Bourrus.

"Why not?"

"I don't know for sure, but I've sometimes wondered whether his home life might have had something to do with it—a wife with an uncontrolled tongue, unconverted and licentious children, and guilt over not acting as a father should toward his family. But Hermas may have thought that the best way to reform the church was by disseminating the revelations he had received rather than by serving within regular church structures. This doesn't mean that he wasn't involved in the life of the Roman church, just that . . . he was a prophet."

"Was he at least supportive of the church?" asked Tavia.

"That's not a simple question," replied Bourrus. "Hermas held onto grand hopes for what the church should become. But he was also acutely aware of how often people—that is, the people who make up the church—fall short of the ideal. You can see both his idealism and his realism in the symbols he uses for the church. For example, in the visions section he compares the church to a woman, but depending upon the message being communicated through the vision, different women appear."

"Or sometimes the same woman changes into a different form," commented Rufina.

"That's right," continued Bourrus. "At one point the church is compared to a fine lady who is holy and wise. At another, an old woman changes into a more youthful woman whose body and hair are still old, but who eventually becomes thoroughly youthful, indicating the changes that can come to the church through repentance. In one instance the church speaks in the voice of a mother instructing her children, but in another is compared to a virgin who is morally pure at her wedding."

"In other words," Rufina carried on, "Hermas envisioned an ideal church, but also recognized that the reality fell considerably short of the ideal. Such awareness is apparent in his parable of the tower. In that parable he envisions building materials for the church. Some are useful, and some not. A builder should not simply throw away materials that do not immediately work for his building project. He knows that some materials will never be usable, but he makes use of anything that can be salvaged for the building."

Polycarp, who thus far was a little less conversational than normal, spoke up. "Hermas was on a mission to change the way the church thought about repentance. He had to wrestle through what to do with a sin he had personally committed after he had been converted and baptized. He looked around the Roman church and noticed that some Christians supported continued participation in the church after a person had committed a sin, as long as that person was repentant. But he also noticed that others in Rome were rigorously advocating purity in the church and contended that someone who sinned after his baptism should be cut off altogether. Hermas was attracted by the message of the rigorists, but also had to deal with the painful truth that he had personally sinned after his own baptism when he had fantasized about being married to a woman who wasn't his wife. His consternation about whether such a sin could be forgiven was resolved, in his view, through the message he received; that is, that sin after baptism could be forgiven as long as the one who had sinned repented—but once, and only once."

"I gather from how you are speaking about this, Polycarp, that you do not entirely agree with this idea," observed Tavia.

"You are correct. I deeply long for holiness in the church of our Lord, and have struggled for the purity of the church my whole life. I believe that one who lives in unrepentant sin as a life pattern is not a true brother or sister. Nevertheless, someone who sins after his incorporation into the church can be forgiven and restored, as long as his repentance is true. You may recall that I held out hope that Valens and his wife would repent when I wrote to the Philippians. Furthermore, I do not believe that this can only happen once."

"Then you don't think he interpreted this message correctly?" asked Tavia.

"My opinion is that Hermas received a true word from God that drew him toward the message of repentance, a message that was given to counteract what the rigorists had been teaching. God intended to encourage Hermas and others with the message that sin committed even after one's baptism could be forgiven. But I think Hermas himself was probably the one who took the further step in claiming that this meant repentance could only happen once," suggested Polycarp. "And in this case I think that this particular prophet took his message too far. As a bishop, it is my responsibility to try to distinguish what is correct from what is not."

"Do you have other concerns about this writing?" asked Tavia.

"Hermas sometimes seemed a bit confused—or perhaps I just don't understand him—about what he meant when he used the word 'spirit.' Sometimes he seemed to be talking about an angel, sometimes the spirit of a human. Other times I think he was writing about the Holy Spirit. But it is often difficult to tell. Furthermore, his intense focus upon repentance in the church, in an ironic way, seems sometimes to distract from a focus on the founder of the church, Jesus Christ. When he does mention Jesus explicitly, he implies that God chose to put the Holy Spirit within the man Jesus on account of the holy and chaste life Jesus had lived on earth to that point."

"That is certainly not the way I would put it," observed Tavia. "Did he explain more fully what he meant?"

"Unfortunately—or fortunately as the case may be—he didn't. So I'm not certain about what he actually believed about the person of Jesus," replied Polycarp. "He doesn't focus much detailed attention on doctrinal matters, so it's difficult to know precisely what he was getting at."

"Is there anything you actually like about this writing?" asked Artemidorus.

"Yes," replied Polycarp. "I appreciate Hermas's emphasis on holiness and his call for people who have sinned to fully and completely repent. I think this message has been helpful in the church. Since this idea shows up so often in the book, I can honestly say that it is something I appreciate about this writing as a whole."

"Anything else?"

"I value Hermas's concern for the poor, and his challenge that those who are rich should generously share with those who are poor. But . . . "

"But what?"

"Hermas promoted a type of reciprocity between the material wealth of the rich and the spiritual wealth of the poor. He compared rich people to a vine. The vine grows up around the poor who are represented by an elm tree. Since rich people are spiritually weak, they need the prayers and confession of the poor who are strong in the Lord to spiritually support them. The rich get supported by the prayers of the poor, while the poor are supported by the money of the rich."

"That's a new concept for me," said Artemidorus.

"And for me as well!" commented Polycarp. "There is one more thing, though, that I appreciate about Hermas's writings," said Polycarp. "Hermas often warned against double-mindedness. He called on those who profess to be Christians to turn to the Lord with all their hearts, to purify their lives of all vanities, and to offer their prayers to God with confidence. He called on God's people to clothe themselves with faith and not allow their minds and hearts to be distracted from focusing on God. I know the pull toward double-mindedness; and I'm sure each of you also knows it as well. I think Hermas's word on this is a good word for each of us today."

The other four nodded their heads in agreement.

Excerpts from
The Shepherd of Hermas

The man who raised me sold me to a certain woman named Rhoda in Rome. Many years later I saw her again and began to love her like a sister. Sometime later I saw her bathing in the Tiber River, and I offered her my hand and helped her out of the river. When I saw her beauty I reasoned in my heart, saying, "How fortunate I would be if I had such a woman of beauty and behavior." Sometime later when I was going toward Cumae and praising God's creatures for being great and remarkable and strong, I fell asleep while I walked. And a spirit took me and carried me through a roadless place through which a man would not be able to pass, for the place was steep and broken up by the waters. When I had crossed the river, I came to level ground and I knelt down and began to pray to the Lord and confess my sins. While I was praying the heavens opened and I saw that woman, the one I had desired, greeting me from heaven, saying, "Greetings, Hermas." And I looked at her and said to her, "Lady, what are you doing here?" And she answered me, "I have been taken up in order that I might expose your sins to the Lord." (Vision 1.1.1–5)

After I had prayed in my house and sat down on the bed a certain man entered, glorious in appearance, in the form of a shepherd, wearing a white hide and carrying a bag on his shoulder and a staff in his hand. He greeted me, and I greeted him in return. He immediately sat down next to me and said to me, "I was sent by the most revered angel to live with you the rest of the days of your life." I thought that he was there to tempt me, so I said to him, "So, who are you? Because I know," I said, "to whom I have been given." He said to me, "Don't you know me?" "No," I replied. "I am the shepherd," he said, "to whom you have been given." (Vision 5.1–3)

"Therefore, the Lord has appointed repentance for those who were called before these days. For since the Lord is the one who knows every heart and everything in advance, he knew the weakness of men and the craftiness of the devil, and that he would do something evil to the servants of God and act wickedly toward them. Therefore, since the Lord is so full of compassion, he showed compassion upon his creation and appointed this repentance—and to me was given authority over this repentance. But I tell you," he said, "after that great and holy call, if anyone is tempted by the devil and sins, he can only repent once. But if he sins repeatedly and repents, it is useless to such a man, for he will barely live." (Commandment 4.3.4–6)

Chapter 8

The Letter of Barnabas

Thursday Evening

"THE LENTIL SOUP IS delicious, Tavia." Polycarp was never short on compliments, but in this case everyone could tell he was enjoying his dinner. He tore off a strip of flat bread, dipped it in the lentils, and commented, "Fresh vegetables, too. How did you manage that?"

"Oh, I have my ways . . . " Tavia smiled. "Actually, at midday someone selling produce came to the door while you were napping. I was able to buy some carrots, onions, garlic, and even a couple of fresh tomatoes—probably all from nearby farms. Today I think I would have paid almost anything for what he was selling."

"That I doubt," retorted Rufina. "I can't imagine you getting anything less than a good price from any seller."

"Not today, I'm afraid. Crocus didn't show up this morning, and I was short on supplies. I was overcharged to be sure, but still thankful for the opportunity to buy some needed staples." She looked over at Polycarp. "I bought some olives to accompany your breakfast tomorrow."

Polycarp beamed in anticipation. He loved his olives.

"But . . . " Tavia paused for a moment before she continued, "the seller seemed overly . . . curious. He was noticeably surprised at how much food I was buying."

At her comment about food consumption, everyone looked at Artemidorus—they couldn't help it. The young man eventually noticed that everyone was staring at him, "What? . . . The seller obviously didn't know that there were five people eating here."

"I'm pretty sure he thought the number was closer to eight!" chuckled Tavia while the others struggled to conceal their amusement. She continued, "I don't think I would have given the seller's curiosity a second thought, except . . . five minutes later I cracked open the door and saw him talking with the woman at the farm house down the road . . . "

"The same woman Crocus talked to yesterday?" asked Rufina.

"The same woman . . . yes. And they kept pointing toward this house. I'm sure of it."

Rufina hesitated and then commented, "That worries me. I didn't want to say anything yesterday—since I make every effort to avoid unkind words about anyone—but . . . I know the woman you're talking about, at least I've talked to her a couple times. She's a meddler. She simply has to know about everybody's business. If that woman really wants to find out what is going on here, she won't stop until she discovers everything she wants to know. Once she knows—actually, before she knows—everyone else also will know."

"Then we have to leave right now!" exclaimed Artemidorus. "We can't risk Polycarp being discovered."

"But leave to where? Where could we go?" asked Rufina.

Bourrus suggested, "I've already given some thought to this. Rufina, you know my sister's summer house? It's only about a thirty minute walk from here. It's small, but it's empty. We could move there temporarily if we had to."

"Then it's settled. Let's pack our things and go!" insisted Artemidorus.

Polycarp placed his hand on Artemidorus's shoulder, "Now hold on for a moment. Is it possible we might be overreacting, even a little bit? A food seller indicates surprise at a larger sale than he expects, and a woman waves her hand in the direction of this house. If we startle at this, we'll jump when somebody sneezes!

Besides, if the authorities are intent on finding me, they eventually will. I won't be able to run forever."

"But ... "

"Artemidorus, I'm willing to move if we must, but I don't see any point in it yet. You need to remember that the helpers of our faith are reverence and patience, and our allies are endurance and self–control."

Tavia commented, "That's a beautiful expression. Where is it from? Did you make it up?"

"It's from the letter of Barnabas," replied Polycarp.

"Barnabas?" she inquired, "as in the Apostle Paul's companion?"

"No," replied Polycarp, "as in Barnabas of Alexandria."

"I don't think I've heard of him," noted Tavia.

"No, you probably haven't. His letter was written about twenty years ago around the time that Hadrian was building a temple to Jupiter in Jerusalem on the site of the destroyed Jewish temple. Since then the letter of Barnabas of Alexandria has sometimes been read in churches in Egypt, but is less–known outside the region."

"Why is that?"

"Probably because Barnabas's approach to interpretation is more common among Christians in Egypt than it is other places."

"Can you explain? You know I'm interested in the process of interpretation."

"Yes, but first let me tell you a little about the letter."

"Thank you!" retorted Artemidorus, who still was tense about the meddlesome neighbor. "Maybe I'll have a chance of following this discussion!"

Polycarp smiled. "Early in his letter, Barnabas mentioned that it was because of love for the sons and daughters of God—by which he meant Christians—that he set out to write. His stated goal was to impart knowledge to his readers so that their faith wouldn't stand alone, but instead would be accompanied by perfect knowledge."

At the mention of perfect knowledge Rufina looked apprehensive, "This Barnabas isn't one of the knowing–ones, is he?"

"No," replied Polycarp, "even though the word 'knowledge' appears in the letter at some key points. And it is worthwhile for you to be aware that the knowing–ones are making headway in Egypt right now. But you can tell that the letter of Barnabas of Alexandria is not one of the writings of the knowing–ones because Barnabas openly shares his knowledge with everyone who will receive it, not just with an elite cadre of those chosen to be in the know."

"So what did he know that he wanted to share?" asked Artemidorus.

"He wanted to show how to interpret Scripture," replied Polycarp.

"Did he really know how?" asked Tavia.

"Let me tell you about the letter, and then you can decide for yourself," answered Polycarp. "Barnabas believed that Christians alone stood at the proper vantage point from which to interpret Scripture."

"I believe that, too," said Tavia.

"And that Jews have consistently misinterpreted their Scriptures," Polycarp added.

"Well, I grant that Jews have missed the most important thing—that Jesus is the promised Messiah—but that doesn't mean all their interpretations are wrong. How could Barnabas make such a claim?" asked Tavia.

"Because Barnabas interpreted everything in Scripture allegorically. Well, maybe not everything. He occasionally interpreted sentences literally and typologically . . . "

"Typologically . . . more like Clement?" interjected Bourrus.

"Yes, like Clement," replied Polycarp. "But Barnabas mostly interpreted using an allegorical approach. Not only did he interpret allegorically, he also aimed at demonstrating that literal Jewish interpretations and applications were not correct."

Artemidorus looked confused, "I'm lost. Typological . . . allegorical . . . ?"

Polycarp laughed, "Since Bourrus just mentioned Clement, maybe if I describe Clement's usual approach to interpretation it will be easier to understand Barnabas's approach. Clement is a good example of someone who interpreted the Scriptures historically for the most part, which for him included typological interpretation, that is, looking for patterns from the past that connect to the present. Since Clement assumed that God's character was the same in every era, he also assumed that God would repeatedly do similar things in successive generations that would show up again and again in various parts of Scripture. In other words, if God did one type of thing in the past, he was likely to do the same type of thing in a later stage of history. There was usually one main point of comparison, and both the original event, any similar intervening events, and the thing he was comparing to all were historically rooted."

"And you're saying that that's typological interpretation," clarified Artemidorus.

"Briefly yes," replied Polycarp.

"So how is that different than allegorical interpretation?" asked the young man.

Polycarp replied, "Allegorical interpretation draws upon texts that were not composed to be allegories and derives alternative interpretations from them than are discoverable in the text itself—different even than you might uncover by comparing a particular text with other similar Scriptures. In other words, allegorical interpretation is not rooted in history the way typological interpretation is. The allegorist assumes that since God is the author of Scripture, there must be a hidden trap door underneath every text that leads to a concealed staircase that you can follow to a secret room that contains deeper meanings that were put there by God for us to find."

"Can you give an example?" asked Artemidorus.

"Yes. You know that Jews avoid eating the meat of pigs, certain birds, and some sea creatures."

Artemidorus nodded his head.

"Barnabas said that food laws about animals by Moses were never intended by God to be taken literally. Those laws require a spiritual interpretation, that is, an allegorical one. Barnabas included a lengthy explanation in his letter about how to interpret such dietary laws. In particular, he claimed that God gave those laws so that his people wouldn't associate with lawless and immoral people who act like the prohibited animals. Instead, they should associate with those who receive God's spiritual food and meditate on it; their associations should be with those who chew on God's teachings like clean animals who chew on the cud."

Tavia asked, "Is Barnabas claiming that such interpretations add additional meaning, or that such interpretations are the real meanings of the text? Is he saying that Jews never should have kept those laws in the first place?"

"He appears to be claiming that his interpretations are the real meanings of the text, and that Jews never should have kept those food laws."

Tavia asked, "But how does Barnabas know his allegorical interpretations are correct? Doesn't allegorical interpretation open the door to someone interpreting a text any way he wants?"

"It certainly can open such a door," answered Polycarp. "Barnabas, though, was constrained by the tradition he had received, which kept him from heading off into doctrinal deviations. He was also restrained by the Christian's hope for the future, by ethical boundaries for what constituted righteous living, and by love, all three of which he mentioned early in his letter."

"Those sound like good boundaries," said Tavia.

Polycarp continued, "But within those constraints, Barnabas considered himself to possess two keys that opened the door into his allegorical interpretations."

"What were those?" asked Rufina.

"His first key was that he knew that Scripture belonged to Christians; so he worked on the assumption that every text had some sort of present application to us. He firmly believed that God had endowed Christians with special insight and understanding of God's hidden wisdom simply because they were Christians, which allowed interpreters like him to look back on events and laws to discern their spiritual meanings."

"And his second key?" asked Rufina.

"His second key was that Jewish interpretations of those same texts must be wrong."

"Now that is where I'm stuck," objected Tavia. "How could Jewish interpreters get all those texts wrong? The prophets themselves were Jewish; they interpreted their mission as calling back the children of Israel to obedience to the covenantal laws God had given them through Moses. I'm starting to wonder if Barnabas's letter was more than just a discussion about how to interpret Scripture. Am I right about this? Was one of his purposes to try to show that Jews were mistaken—that their special place as God's children had been taken over by the church?"

"That's certainly how it looks to me," replied Polycarp. "Still, Barnabas's primary purpose was not to bad-mouth Jewish people, but instead to demonstrate that Christians were the true heirs of the Scriptures and so possessed the privilege of interpreting those Scriptures in a Christian way."

"This gives me a lot to think about," said Tavia.

"My head is starting to hurt," said Artemidorus. "Do many people interpret allegorically?"

"Yes, a lot of people do," replied Polycarp, "but Alexandria is especially known for its allegorizing. For some time now Greeks inside and outside of Alexandria have been interpreting Homer and Hesiod allegorically. And more than a hundred years ago a famous Alexandrian Jew named Philo popularized allegorical interpretation of the Jewish Scriptures."

"Don't forget the knowing-ones," interjected Rufina. "They allegorize too. And, as you already pointed out, there are plenty of knowing-ones in Egypt."

"But what about Christians like us? Do we allegorize?" asked Artemidorus.

"Some of us do, and some don't. I'll admit that it creates difficulties when those of us who don't sit down in the same room with those who do," said Polycarp.

Bourrus said, "Polycarp, as I remember, there are significant similarities between the end of this document and the beginning of the document from Syria. Is that correct?"

"Yes, that is correct. Barnabas's letter ends with a discussion of the two ways, the way of life and the way of death, just like the document from Syria we talked about yesterday morning. There are so many similarities between the beginning of the Syrian document and the end of Barnabas's letter that it is obvious that the two documents somehow drew upon the same traditional teachings."

There was a break in the discussion, and it seemed clear that this conversation was coming to an end. So Polycarp changed the subject, "Tavia, is there any chance I could trouble you for one of those olives right now . . . as a foretaste of tomorrow's breakfast?" He smiled mischievously. "Perhaps there is a deeper interpretation that can be drawn from . . . a green olive? Olives can expose the true nature of people, and are a token of the future. Some people love green olives while others are repulsed by them. The true meaning of the green olive . . . " Polycarp grinned when he emphasized the word *true*, " . . . and the reason God gave us green olives in the first place—was to establish a permanent sign to distinguish those who have developed a taste for heavenly realities from those who have not. This is an allegorical symbol for all of us. Let the one with understanding understand."

Tavia smiled at Polycarp's allegorical satire. But recognizing its true purpose, she stood up to fetch a plate of olives for her beloved teacher.

Excerpts from The Letter of Barnabas

I figured that if I care enough about you to share a bit of what I have received, there will be a reward for me for ministering to such spirits. So I have been diligent to send you this brief message, that along with your faith you might have perfect knowledge. There are, then, three basic doctrines of the Lord: the hope of life (the beginning and end of our faith), righteousness (the beginning and end of judgment), and love (a testimony of gladness and rejoicing in works of righteousness). For the Master made known to us through the prophets things that happened, things that are happening now, and has given us a foretaste of things that are about to happen. (1.5–7a)

What does he say? "Into the good land, a land flowing with milk and honey." Blessed be our Lord, brothers and sisters, who has placed in us wisdom and understanding of his secrets. For the prophet speaks a parable of the Lord. Who can understand it except the one who is wise and understanding and loves his Lord? Since he renewed us by the forgiveness of sins, he made us another type, as though we had the soul of children, as if he were forming us again. (6.10–11)

Moses says again, "Eat anything that has a divided hoof and chews the cud." What is he saying? That the animal who receives the food knows the one who feeds it, and since the animal depends upon him seems to rejoice. He saw the commandment and spoke correctly. What, then, is he saying? Associate with those who fear the Lord, with those who meditate in their heart on the special message they received, with those who speak and keep the righteous requirements of the Lord, with those who know that meditation is a joyful endeavor and who repeatedly chew on the word of the Lord. But what is the divided hoof? It means that the righteous person both walks in this world and is waiting expectantly for the holy age to come. Notice how appropriately Moses gave these laws! But how could those people understand or comprehend these things? But since we correctly understand the commandments, we speak as the Lord intended. This is why he circumcised our ears and our hearts, that we might understand these things. (10.11–12)

But let us move on to other knowledge and teaching. There are two ways of teaching and authority, one of light and one of darkness, and there is a great difference between the two ways. For over one are appointed light-carrying angels of God, but over the other are angels of Satan. On one side is the Lord who is from eternity to eternity, but on the other is the ruler of the present time of lawlessness. (18.1–2)

Chapter 9

Second Clement

Friday Morning

" . . . TO THE ONLY invisible God, the Father of truth, who sent to us the Savior and Originator of immortality, through whom he revealed to us truth and heavenly life, to him be the glory forever and ever. Amen."

The other four responded to their bishop's morning prayer with a hearty "Amen!" Conversation started slowly, but eventually veered in the direction of various sermons that had impacted them over the years. Tavia asked, "Polycarp, are there any sermons after the time of the apostles that have been written down? I know that most sermons are spoken to individual congregations at particular moments, but if any have been written down, I'd be interested in reading them."

"There is one sermon I know in written form," replied Polycarp. "In fact, I was just now quoting from the doxology of that sermon at the end of my prayer."

"How can you quote like that? You know how amazing that is, don't you? Where did you get such an incredible memory?" exclaimed Artemidorus.

"The Lord has granted me the ability to remember well, and I thank him for it," Polycarp replied to Artemidorus. Then to Tavia he said, "I don't know much about the background of this sermon.

I don't even know the name of the elder who spoke it or where it was spoken. Bourrus, do you have any recollection of where we acquired the copy we have in Smyrna?"

"Yes. We made a request to Corinth many years ago for a copy of Clement's letter to keep in our archives. Do you remember that?"

"Yes."

"A scribe in Corinth copied the sermon you're talking about at the same time."

"Do you know where it was originally spoken?" asked Rufina.

"No. I only know that it was copied together with Clement's letter. Polycarp, do you have any additional information?"

Polycarp replied, "The sermon itself suggests that it was addressed to Christians who grew up as pagans rather than as Jews. The preacher reminds his listeners that before their salvation, their minds had been blinded because they worshiped objects made out of stones, wood, gold, silver, and brass."

"Anything else?" asked Bourrus.

Polycarp responded, "There is one section in the sermon that suggests it was delivered at a special meeting of believers from various house churches who came together to hear messages from several elders."

"Then why do we just have this sermon," asked Rufina, "if other sermons were preached at the same time?"

"Because this particular sermon was written down before it was spoken," replied Polycarp.

"That's unusual. Why go to all the effort to write it down before speaking it?" asked Rufina. "That would entail an enormous amount of work for a single sermon, even if it was planned for a larger gathering of believers."

Bourrus the scribe turned and addressed Rufina, "As you know, my dear wife, some of us are more comfortable writing than speaking. Maybe the elder knew ahead of time that he was going to deliver this message and wanted to make sure that he had all his thoughts in order before he opened his mouth in front of so many people."

Rufina paused, and then nodded understandingly at her scholarly husband.

Tavia asked, "So what's the sermon about?"

"The sermon focuses upon repentance and self–control," said Polycarp. "Really, it touches upon various topics connected to righteous living, but keeps coming back to the themes of repentance and self–control as qualities that should figure prominently in the lives of Christians."

"What methods did he use to motivate them?" asked Tavia.

Polycarp responded, "There were a couple different ways this elder tried to persuade his listeners to emphasize repentance and self–control. The first way was by focusing his message upon the future. This elder sought to impress upon his listeners that the Lord would return soon, even though no one knew the day of his appearing. He compared the present age with the age to come. At the end of time, he said, the Lord will gather together all nations, tribes, and languages, and render judgment according to their deeds. There will be a resurrection followed by a judgment of fire as hot as a blazing furnace, and everyone's works, both private and public, will be revealed. We as Christians should not be grieved if we experience sadness in the present time, said the preacher, since there will be a time of true blessedness in the future. He also said that we should practice righteousness in the present age so that we will be saved in the age to come. As we wait for that day, we need to love one another and thereby be prepared to enter the future kingdom of God."

"I'm motivated by those kinds of reminders," said Tavia. "I want to be ready when the Lord returns. I deeply desire to live my life now in light of his future coming."

The others in the room nodded their heads in agreement.

"You said that there were two ways he tried to persuade them to repent and live in self–control," said Tavia. "What was the other way?"

"The elder who delivered this sermon quoted a lot from those who had gone before him. He called upon his listeners to submit to the word that had already been spoken. He wanted the people who heard him to pay special attention to what had already been written."

"Where were his quotations from?" asked Tavia.

"He repeatedly drew quotations from all three of our sources of authority," replied Polycarp, "from the prophets who announced in advance the coming of Christ, from the earthly teachings of the Lord himself, and from the apostles who preached the gospel to us. He was familiar with a lot of Scripture, and quoted it often."

"Like you, Polycarp," said Artemidorus proudly.

Polycarp continued, "The fact that he quoted so much Scripture in his sermon may be a primary reason it continues to be copied and used among Christians. But the preacher didn't always seem to know the sources of his quotations."

"And you usually do," observed Artemidorus.

"Yes, usually . . . " replied Polycarp. "Among his quotations, the elder included a few sayings of the Lord I've never heard. And, to tell the truth, I'm uncertain about the genuineness of a couple of them. Considering how many inauthentic words of Jesus are disseminated by the knowing-ones these days, I think we might have to ignore a couple sayings this preacher claims are from the Lord unless we can find support for them in other well-established streams of the apostolic tradition."

"That seems wise," said Rufina. "Many are being led astray these days."

"Since I've mentioned the knowing-ones, I should point out that I'm pretty sure that the preacher countered them at various moments in his sermon, even though he doesn't address them directly. For example, this elder emphasized that Christ our savior actually became flesh, that the church is a fleshly copy of the spiritual church, that individuals in it can receive the Spirit in their fleshly bodies, and that our future resurrection will be in the flesh."

"Fleshly language like that would make the knowing-ones choke on their olives," said Artemidorus. "It's good he emphasized that."

"Do you have any concerns about this elder's doctrine? Would you recommend that it be used in our churches?" inquired Tavia.

"My only concern," replied Polycarp, "is how much stress this elder placed upon the actions of humans for attaining final salvation. He put so much emphasis on human actions that he seemed sometimes to lose sight of the truth that it is by grace we have been saved. It is not of works, but by the will of God through Jesus Christ."

"Specifically?" asked Tavia.

"A good example of his overemphasis on human action is the preacher's claim that fasting is better than prayer, and that giving money to the poor is better than either fasting or prayer. He regularly overemphasized the righteous actions of humans for salvation and underemphasized the actions of God. Now, the preacher may simply have been assuming that his listeners knew the close connection between faith and repentance, but his words tended to highlight the need for Christians to focus on self-control as an essential element of repentance rather than on God's part in drawing people to that repentance through faith."

"That's interesting," commented Tavia. "I would love to pursue a discussion of what God does versus what we do in relationship to salvation at some point. Would you be open to that?"

"Of course, Tavia. Just keep the olives coming!"

Artemidorus interrupted. "What's that sound? Someone's outside . . . running." Just then there was an insistent knocking on the door.

Tavia walked to the door, opened it a crack, and then threw it open, "Alce . . . Anthousa . . . ? What are you doing here, little sisters? Don't you know it's dangerous for you? What will your mistress say about your being gone?"

"We have a long list . . . of errands," replied one of the young slaves. "Our mistress . . . won't expect us until . . . evening. We had to . . . warn you . . . "

"You're both out of breath. Come in, sit down, and tell us what's wrong," said Rufina.

"No, there's no time! You have to leave . . . right away."

"What happened?"

Alce caught her breath first, "Crocus betrayed Polycarp."

"What?" said Artemidorus. "How do you know?"

"We heard him," said Anthousa.

"Actually, we saw him first," said Alce.

"And then we heard him," said Anthousa.

"We saw him talking to the constable," said Alce.

"We couldn't understand why he would do that," said Anthousa.

"Since he was supposed to be hiding your whereabouts," said Alce.

"So we moved closer," said Anthousa.

"Behind a wall," added Alce.

"And we heard him," said Anthousa.

"Heard him say what?" insisted Artemidorus.

"We heard him describe the location of the country house," said Alce.

"In detail," added Anthousa.

"No!" exclaimed Artemidorus. "I knew something was wrong with Crocus!"

"They had an agreement . . . " said Alce.

" . . . that the constable wouldn't tell anyone how he found out," said Anthousa.

"But we heard him!" insisted Alce.

"Yes, we heard him!" said Anthousa adamantly.

"And you have to go . . . now," said Alce. "We think the authorities are already on their way."

The others said nothing at first, but instead looked over at Polycarp who was still seated at the table. The elderly man rose and made his way over to the two young slaves. He placed one hand on the head of each girl and said, "Blessings upon each of you, my little sisters in the Lord. Thank you for being servants of your heavenly Master today. Thank you for bringing us this message. May the Lord bless you for it, and richly reward you. May he protect you from harm."

He looked up at the others and said, "So what should we do?"

"Is there any question?" spouted Artemidorus. "Let's go, right now!"

Tavia nodded in agreement, and so did Bourrus and Rufina. Bourrus directed, "We'll go to my sister's place. It's small, but it's isolated."

"Quickly, then," said Rufina. "Gather your things. Let's make it look like no one was ever here."

"No, auntie Rufina!" said Alce, "You go! All of you. . . . Take Polycarp and the others. Take whatever you can carry. Leave Anthousa and me to pick up everything else. We know how to work fast. We can be out of here in half an hour."

Polycarp looked uncertain, but Rufina asserted herself, "Yes, that's a good plan. We must go now." She spoke to Alce and Anthousa, "Thank you, dear sisters," then to everyone else, "Carry whatever you can. Let's be out the door as soon as possible. Artemidorus, help Polycarp with his sandals."

Ten minutes later, they were on their way.

Excerpts from Second Clement

So, brothers and sisters, since we have renounced our residence in this world, let us do the will of the one who called us and not be afraid to leave this world. For the Lord says, "You will be like lambs among wolves." (5.1–2)

Let none of you say that this flesh is not judged and does not rise again. Consider this: In what state were you saved? In what state did you regain your sight, if it was not while you were in this flesh? Therefore we must protect the flesh as a temple of God. For as you were called in the flesh, so also you will come in the flesh. If Christ the Lord who saved us became flesh and called us in that state, even though he was spirit first, we also in the flesh will receive the reward. (9.1–5)

So, brothers and sisters, since we have received no small opportunity to repent, while there is still time let us turn again to the God who called us since we still have one who accepts us. For if we forsake these comforts and conquer our soul by not doing its evil desires we will share in mercy from Jesus. But you know that the day of judgment is already coming like a burning furnace, and some of the heavens will dissolve, and all the earth will melt like lead in a fire, and then the secret and open works of men will be exposed. Giving to the poor, like repenting from sin, is good. Fasting is better than prayer, giving to the poor is better than either, love covers a multitude of sins, and prayer coming out of a good conscience rescues from death. Blessed is everyone who is found to be full of these, for giving to the poor lightens the weight of sin. (16.1–4)

So let us help each other to restore those who are particularly weak in goodness, that we all may be saved, and let us turn back and warn one another. Let us think about paying attention and believing not only now while we are being warned by the elders; let us also remember the Lord's commands and not allow ourselves to get dragged away by worldly desires when we have gone home. Let us come here more often and try to advance in the commands of the Lord, so that in unity of mind we all might be gathered into life. For the Lord said, "I am coming to gather all the nations, tribes, and languages." This is a reference to the day of his appearing, when he will come and redeem us, each according to his works. And the unbelievers will see his glory, and they will be amazed when they see the kingdom of the world belongs to Jesus, saying, "Woe to us, because it was you, and we did not know it nor believe. We did not obey the elders who preached to us about our salvation." And their worm will not die and their fire will not be extinguished, and they will be a spectacle for all flesh. (17.2–5)

Chapter 10

To Diognetus

Friday Evening

"WE MUST PRAY FOR kings and judges and rulers and for everyone who persecutes and hates us. We must pray for the enemies of the cross, in the hope that the fruit of our faith might become obvious to everyone, and that we might be perfected in him." Polycarp's face evinced a deep serenity, and his eyes exuded a committed trust in the One he served. Polycarp's companions would later remember the way he radiated trust in the midst of impending calamity.

Still, Artemidorus could not hide his consternation, "Why are we hated by the world? We love each other. We forgive those who wrong us. We pay our taxes. We exhort each other not to lie, steal, or commit adultery. Why can't they understand us?"

Polycarp addressed his young assistant, "That is a good question, but it cannot be answered simply. Maybe this would be an appropriate time for us to continue our discussion of Christian writings. I know a document that offers some answers to this question."

"But, Polycarp, we only arrived a few hours ago," said Rufina, "and you must be tired from our rush to get here. Perhaps we should forgo this discussion until a later time."

"Who can predict whether there will be a later time?" responded Polycarp. "Besides, the text I'm thinking of is splendid.

It attractively describes Christians encountering a world in which they often face suspicion and hostility."

Bourrus looked up in anticipation, since he was pretty sure he had just figured out which document Polycarp was referring to. It was one of his favorite writings—at least among those writings that had been composed during his lifetime. "The apology for Diognetus . . . that's the one you're talking about, isn't it?"

"Precisely," said Polycarp.

"Diognetus?" inquired Tavia. "Who was Diognetus?"

"All I know about the background of this writing," replied Polycarp, "is that it is addressed to a 'most excellent' Diognetus. Does that expression tell you anything about the recipient?"

"It tells me that Diognetus was probably someone of importance in society, perhaps a government official, or maybe connected to a powerful family," replied Tavia.

"That's right," agreed Polycarp. "And such an assumption fits the skillful rhetoric found in it and the topics addressed throughout. It seems that Diognetus had a number of questions about Christianity he wanted answered."

"Such as?" asked Artemidorus.

"What god do Christians believe in? How do Christians worship this god? Why do they disregard the world? Why do Christians despise death? Why don't they recognize the gods of the Greeks? How are Christians different from Jews? What is this love they claim to have for each other? Why would someone be attracted by such a new religion?"

"Those are a lot of questions!" remarked Artemidorus.

"Yes they are," replied Polycarp. "But in the midst of his answers, the author—or perhaps it would be better to call him a speaker—marvelously describes how Christians live, or at least are supposed to live in the world."

"Who is the author—or should I say speaker," asked Tavia, "and why did you refer to him as a speaker instead of as an author?"

"I don't know who he was, but he clearly was a true brother in the Lord. The reason I called him a speaker is that the document itself suggests that it was composed to be spoken—perhaps at some sort of gathering initiated by Diognetus."

"So how should we live our lives in a world that is often antagonistic and unreceptive to our message?" asked Artemidorus. "When people discover I'm a Christian, they often assume all sorts of things about me that aren't true."

"Like what?" asked Rufina.

"You know as well as I do . . . probably better," replied Artemidorus.

"Of course I do. But you're newer at this than I am, so I'd like to hear what people are saying about you . . . that is, about us."

"That we're atheists because we don't sacrifice to their gods; that we eat human flesh and engage in sexual orgies at our love feasts; that we're trying to subvert the government . . . "

Rufina responded, "I've heard all of these. And I won't deny that there are lots of untrue stories circulating about us. It's hard enough facing a direct accusation that you're a Christian; but it's much harder when accusations brought against you are false. Unfortunately for us a lot of pressures Christians face these days come from being falsely accused."

Polycarp picked it up, "Fortunately for us the speaker of this document set out to answer a few of the misconceptions people have about Christians, and to recommend Christianity to those who desire to understand our beliefs and way of life."

"Tell us more," said Artemidorus.

"After listing the questions that Diognetus wanted answered, the speaker appealed to him to reconsider whether gods made out of stone, bronze, wood, or silver really were anything at all. Before such objects were carved or cast, he explained, the craftsman who made them theoretically could have decided to fashion from his materials something besides an object of worship. If he could have formed something totally different from what he actually formed, then how can the things he made be gods? They are deaf and blind; they rot and rust. Besides, if they're really gods, why do people leave their cheap stone and pottery gods out in the open, but lock away their gold and silver gods at night? Can't gods protect themselves?"

"This sounds like a critique Isaiah or one of the other prophets would have made," commented Rufina.

"Yes, it's very similar." Polycarp continued, "After showing the folly of pagan idol worship, the speaker goes on to differentiate Christians from Jews. The God of the Jews is the true God, he said, but Jewish sacrifices are no better than pagan sacrifices, since the reason Jews offer sacrifices is that they think God needs them. God doesn't need sacrifices; he created heaven and earth—why would he need anything at all?

"Moreover, the food laws of the Jews are obviously unneeded—why would God create such food in the first place if he didn't expect us to eat it? He said that their sabbaths are misguided—why would God forbid us to do good on a particular day of the week? And circumcision is unnecessary—how can mutilating the flesh be a sign of God's election? The speaker argued that Christians are not like Jews in these matters."

"Maybe that's why it feels like nobody understands us," commented Artemidorus. "Greeks assume that our rejection of their gods is silly and impious; Jews think we are simply disobeying what God has told us to do."

"I'm afraid you're right," agreed Polycarp. "Christians are distinct from both Greeks and Jews, and some of the pressure is caused by our differences. But the speaker not only showed that we are dissimilar to pagans and Jews, he described us as a different race altogether. Even though you can't recognize Christians by the language they speak or by their cultural habits, Christians possess a different character than other people in the world. They are citizens of a different country—a heavenly one—and reside everywhere in this world as though they were foreigners. The speaker compared Christians living in the world to a person's soul. The soul dwells in the body, but is not of the body; likewise Christians dwell in the world, but are not of the world."

"That's another reason we're disliked by the world," said Artemidorus. "We don't go along with their immoral practices."

"The speaker addressed that topic, too," said Polycarp. "He explained that Christians are often hated by the world even though

Christians try not to harm others. We receive ridicule and abuse because we are an obstacle to people who want to indulge their pleasures."

"Don't I know it . . . " agreed Artemidorus.

"Did he talk about Jesus?" asked Tavia. "Did he introduce Diognetus to our Lord?"

"Yes, but the speaker presented Jesus in a way that he thought might be easier for Diognetus to receive. He said that the Creator communicated his word to humans and fixed it in their hearts, not by sending an angel or a human ruler, but by sending himself. The speaker compared what God did to a king sending his son, who was also co–regent, as his representative. In sending his son, it was like sending himself. But the king who traveled to our world came not for tyranny, but for love . . . as one calling, not pursuing . . . as one loving, not judging."

"Did the speaker explain how Diognetus could become a Christian?" asked Tavia.

"Yes. The speaker explained that people are unable to enter the kingdom of God on their own because they have sinned. The wages of sin is punishment and death. But God in his great mercy gave his own son to be our ransom. The son took our place—the holy one for the lawless, the guiltless for the guilty, the just for the unjust, the incorruptible for the corruptible, the immortal for the mortal. It was only in him that we could be justified in God's sight. The only means by which any of us will ever be permitted to see God is by exercising faith in what God has revealed."

"I am so glad that I'm a citizen of this kingdom," said Artemidorus. "It's actually amazing that God could love and accept someone like me."

"I'm thankful that God saved you as well, my young friend," replied Polycarp.

Tavia asked, "Polycarp, do you know whether Diognetus received this message positively? Do you know how he reacted to it?"

"I'm afraid I do not know," replied Polycarp. "But I do know that the speaker urged him to come to faith. He explained that it was out of God's love for the people of the world—people like

Diognetus—that God sent his only Son. He invited this influential man to become a lover and imitator of God. He told him that he could live as a citizen of heaven, even though his current lot was on earth. He said that as a believer Diognetus's life would become different and that he would begin declaring the mysteries of God. He even said that in time Diognetus would come to understand why Christians are so willing to suffer. Actually, it went beyond that: the speaker told him that if he entered into faith, not only would he understand Christian suffering, he would come to love, admire, and bless those who endure this temporary fire."

At the mention of fire, there was an uncomfortable pause as everyone remembered Polycarp's vision of fire only a couple days past.

But Polycarp had no intention of letting the conversation go there. Instead, like a father who knows he may soon face separation from his children, he looked around tenderly at his four companions and raised his voice in prayer toward heaven: "I ask you, Father of our Lord Jesus Christ, that the eternal high priest, the Son of God Jesus Christ, might build up these four precious souls in faith and truth and gentleness and patience and steadfastness and endurance and purity. May they find a portion and a place among your saints, and I along with them. My prayer is not for these four alone, but also for everyone under heaven who will yet believe in our Lord Jesus Christ and in his Father who raised him from the dead."

There was a hushed silence. For a long time nobody spoke.

Finally Polycarp said, "It is time for me to retire to my room upstairs. I'll see you, precious friends, in the morning . . . if the Lord wills."

Excerpts from To Diognetus

Most excellent Diognetus, I see that you are eager to learn about the religion of the Christians, and that you are specifically and carefully inquiring about them. "What God do they believe in and how do they worship him? How is it that they all disregard the world and don't care about death? How come they don't recognize the gods considered to be gods by the Greeks? Why don't they observe the religious scruples of the Jews? What is this loving affection they have for each other? Why has this new race or way of life come into existence now and not previously?" I welcome your interest, and I ask God, the one who enables us both to speak and to hear, to grant me to speak in such a way that you might best be able to hear, and that you may hear in such a way that the speaker may not have any regrets. (1.1–2)

For Christians cannot be distinguished from the rest of humanity by country or language or custom. They do not live in cities of their own; they do not speak a strange dialect; they do not practice an odd way of life. This teaching of theirs has not been discovered through the thinking and reflection of inquisitive people, nor do they promote any human doctrine like some people do. Although they live in Greek and non–Greek cities, as each one's lot was cast, and follow local customs in dress and diet and the rest of daily life, they also exhibit the remarkable and admittedly peculiar nature of their own citizenship. They live in their own countries, but still as foreigners. They participate as citizens in everything, but endure everything as strangers. Every foreign land is their home country, and every home country is a foreign land. They marry like everyone else and have children, but they do not throw away their off-spring. They share their food table, but not their marriage bed. They happen to be in the flesh, but they do not live according to the flesh. They spend time on earth, but their citizenship is in heaven. (5.1–9)

But when our unrighteousness was fulfilled, and it had become entirely obvious that its wages—punishment and death—were to be expected, God's appointed time to demonstrate his goodness and power arrived at last. Oh, the amazing kindness and love of God! He did not hate us, or reject us, or hold a grudge against us. Rather, he was patient and forbearing. In his mercy he himself took our sins. He gave up his own son as a ransom for us, the holy for the lawless, the innocent for the guilty, the righteous for the unrighteous, the incorruptible for the corruptible, the immortal for the mortal. What else could cover our sins except his righteousness? In whom could we, the lawless and the ungodly, be made righteous except in the Son of God alone? (9.2–4)

Chapter 11

The Martyrdom of Polycarp

"I can't believe he's gone," said Tavia.

"I know," said Rufina, who comfortingly placed her hand on Tavia's shoulder. "I keep expecting to look over and find him sitting at the table."

"I can't stop thinking about his prayers," said Artemidorus. "Again and again in my mind I hear him praying for me . . . and for the three of you . . . and for so many others. I used to listen outside his door while he was praying. I probably shouldn't have done that—and I never told anyone until now—but the memory of those prayers still affect me. It's difficult to express how much I learned about the ways of God simply by listening to him pray."

"I miss his wisdom," said Tavia. "He was an extraordinary guide. I learned from him how to think about and defend what I believe. He was so unselfish with his time—and so generous in sharing the faithful words he received from those who went before him."

"I'm going to miss listening to him quote those long passages—out of the prophets or one of Paul's letters—or even from some obscure document I've never heard of!" said Bourrus. "Nobody will forget his astonishing memory."

Rufina said, "I keep thinking about the time the four of us spent with him, caring for him during his final days . . . and learning so much from him in such a short time. This is the first time just the four of us have been together since his passing, isn't it?"

"I'm very glad to be with you three; I find it comforting," said Tavia. "Rufina, how are our little sisters, Alce and Anthousa?"

"They're fine, all things considered," said Rufina. "This is not the first time those girls have been roughly treated, though never before at the hands of soldiers, and never when a person's life was at risk. For them, it probably won't be the last time they face harsh treatment, unless we can somehow manage to get them discharged from their slavery. Bourrus and I have begun working on that; but it's complicated, as you know."

Tavia wanted to know more. "And Alce in particular? How is she doing?—since she was the one they forced to disclose our final location?"

"I'm spending as much time with her as I am allowed," said Rufina. "She knows that we understand what she endured for Christ and that no one holds any ill will toward her. As you might expect, at first she blamed herself. But she also now understands that Polycarp was certain to be discovered anyway. Alce is a sincere and fervent Christian. I believe that God has good purposes for her in the future."

Tavia was about to ask one more question about Alce, but thought better of it. She looked over at Bourrus, "How is your text for Philomelium coming? I heard that you and the other elders were nearly finished. Is that correct?"

"We are mostly finished," replied Bourrus. "But before it's completed, I wanted to read a portion of it aloud to all of you—the part of the narrative that contains the events closest to the four of us. Would that be alright with you?"

"Yes, please do!" exclaimed all the others, almost in unison.

But Bourrus wanted to explain some things first. "In writing this account, we have made every effort to portray the suffering and execution of our dear bishop as a martyrdom that conforms to the gospel. Wherever we discerned parallels to Jesus' own suffering and death, we were careful to include them. But even when there were no parallels—as happened at a number of points—we still tried to show that Polycarp suffered according to the will of God, kept seeking to proclaim the gospel of God in the midst of his sufferings, and was steadfast in faith until the end. While I'm reading, ask yourselves whether we have demonstrated in our account that our deceased leader's martyrdom was in accordance with the gospel."

"Are you going to read it all to us?" asked Artemidorus.

"No," replied Bourrus. "For now I'll skip the introduction and the portions about Germanicus and Quintus, since the details of those stories are well-known in our community. Instead let me start with the section of the story when our band of four was appointed to watch over Polycarp during his final days, and then read as far as we have completed thus far. As you know, after our brother Germanicus was killed, the crowd started shouting for the authorities to find Polycarp. I'll begin with Polycarp's response and read from there."

Now the most admirable Polycarp was not dismayed when he first heard about it, but wanted to stay in the city. But the others convinced him to leave. So he went out to a little country house not far from the city and stayed there with a few friends. Night and day he did nothing but pray for everyone, and for the churches around the world, as was his usual practice.

While praying he had a vision three days before his arrest and saw his pillow blazing with fire. He turned and said to those with him, "It is necessary for me to be burned alive."

Since they kept searching for him, he moved to another country house. But almost at once his pursuers arrived. When they didn't find him, they seized two young slaves, one of whom confessed under torture. For it really was impossible for him to stay hidden, since those who betrayed him were from his own household. And the chief constable, who just happened to have the same name as Herod, was determined to bring him into the stadium—that Polycarp might fulfill his appointed destiny by becoming a partner with Christ, while those who betrayed him receive the punishment of Judas himself.

They took the young slave with them. It was Friday around the time of the evening meal. The pursuers headed out, mounted on horses and brandishing their regular weapons as though they were pursuing an armed rebel. Closing in on him late that evening, they found him in bed in a little upstairs room. He still could have escaped from there to another place, but he was unwilling. "May God's will be done," he said.

When he heard that they had arrived, he went downstairs and talked to them. Those who were present were amazed at his age and composure, and wondered at the insistence that such an old man be arrested. Right away he ordered food and drink be set before them at that hour—as much as they wanted—but he requested that they give him an hour to pray undisturbed. When they consented, he stood and prayed. He was so full of the grace of God that for two hours he was unable to stop speaking, to the amazement of those who heard. Many regretted that they had come after such a godly old man.

He finally finished his prayer, a prayer in which he remembered everyone he had ever met, whether small or great, well-known or unknown, as well as all those of the true church throughout the world. The time to depart had come, so they seated him on a donkey and brought him into the city, on the day of the great Sabbath. The chief constable, Herod, along with his father, Nicetes, came out to meet him. After transferring him to their carriage, they sat beside him and tried to persuade him, saying, "Why, what's so bad about saying, 'Caesar is Lord,' offering the incense, doing whatever else is required, and so saving yourself?"

Now at first he didn't answer them. But when they persisted, he said, "I am not about to do what you want me to do." So since they failed to persuade him, they started to threaten him. They hurried him out of the carriage so fast that he bruised his shin. But without even turning around—as if nothing had happened—he went along with them willingly and resolutely as they led him to the stadium. When he came into the stadium, the uproar was so intense that no one could hear anything.

But as Polycarp entered the stadium, a voice from heaven came to him, "Be strong, Polycarp—be a man!" No one saw the speaker, but our people who were there heard the voice.

When he was finally brought forward, there was a huge uproar when they heard that Polycarp had been arrested. After he was brought forward, the proconsul asked whether he was Polycarp. When he confessed that he was, the proconsul tried to persuade him to recant, saying, "Have respect for your age," and all the other things they usually say: "Swear by the genius of Caesar! Turn away! Say 'Away with the atheists!'"

Polycarp looked solemnly at the whole crowd of lawless heathen who were in the stadium, motioned toward them with his hand, then groaned as he looked toward heaven and said, "Away with the atheists!"

But the proconsul was insistent, and said, "Swear the oath and I will let you go! Revile Christ!"

Polycarp replied, "Eighty-six years I have served him, and he has never wronged me. How can I blaspheme my King who saved me?"

But the proconsul continued to insist, saying, "Swear by the genius of Caesar!" So Polycarp replied, "If you vainly expect that I will swear by the genius of Caesar, as you say, and pretend that you do not know who I am, then listen carefully: I am a Christian. Now if you want to learn the teaching of Christianity, appoint a day, and give me a proper hearing."

The proconsul replied: "Persuade the people."

But Polycarp said, "You I could count worthy of a response, for we have been taught to appropriately respect rulers and authorities appointed by God as long as it does us no harm. As to bringing a defense to them, I do not consider them worthy."

The proconsul said, "I have wild beasts. I will throw you to them unless you turn away!"

He said, "Call them. Repentance from better to worse is impossible for us; but it is good to turn away from those things that are evil and toward those that are righteous."

Again he said to him, "I will have you consumed by fire since you don't care about wild beasts. Unless you turn!"

Polycarp replied, "You threaten with fire that burns for an hour then soon is extinguished, for you do not know about the coming *judgment and the eternal punishment reserved for the ungodly. So why do you delay? Bring on what you want."*

As he spoke these and many other words, he was filled with courage and joy, and his face was filled with grace. So not only did he not collapse in terror at the things said to him, but on the contrary, the proconsul was astonished, and sent his own herald into the middle of the stadium to announce three times: "Polycarp has confessed that he is a Christian."

When this was announced by the herald, the entire crowd— both Gentiles and Jews who lived in Smyrna—cried out with uncontrollable anger and loud shouting, "This is the teacher of Asia, the father of the Christians, the destroyer of our gods, who tells many not to sacrifice or worship!" They said such things and shouted demands that Philip the Asiarch let loose a lion on Polycarp. But he said that it was not lawful for him to do so because the animal sports were already finished. Then it occurred to them to shout at the same time for Polycarp to be burned alive. For it was necessary that the vision he had received about his pillow be fulfilled—when he was praying and saw it burning and then turned and spoke prophetically to the believers with him, "It is necessary that I be burned alive."

Then everything happened so quickly, quicker than can be told—the crowds hastily gathering wood and kindling from the workshops and baths—the Jews, as usual, being especially eager to assist. When the pyre was ready, he removed all his clothes and took off his belt. He also tried to take off his own shoes, even though he was not used to doing so since the believers always vied with each other to be the first to touch his skin. For he had always been honored—even before his martyrdom—for his holy life. Right away, the materials for the fire were placed around him. They were about to nail him, but he said, "Leave me like this, for the one who gives strength to endure the fire will also give me strength to remain unmoved on the pyre without the security you get from nails."

So they did not nail him, but tied him instead. After his hands were tied behind him, he looked like a splendid ram from a great flock, a burnt offering ready and acceptable to God. He gazed toward heaven and spoke:

"Lord God Almighty,

Father of your beloved and blessed Son Jesus Christ,

through whom we have received knowledge of you,

God of angels and powers and every created thing,

and of the whole race of the righteous who live in your presence.

I bless you because you have counted me worthy of this day and hour,

to take a place among the number of the martyrs in the cup of your Christ,

to the resurrection of eternal life,

both of soul and body,

in the incorruptibility of the Holy Spirit.

May I be received among them in your presence today

as a rich and acceptable sacrifice,

just as you previously prepared and now have fulfilled,

oh undeceiving and true God.

I praise you for this and for everything.

I bless you, I glorify you,

through the eternal and heavenly high priest, Jesus Christ, your beloved Son,

through whom to you with him and the Holy Spirit

be glory both now and in the ages to come. Amen."

When he had offered up the "Amen" and finished the prayer, the men attending to the fire lit it. As the great flame blazed we saw a miracle (that is, we to whom it was given to see). We have been preserved so that we can relate to others what happened. For the fire took the shape of an arch, like the sail of a ship filled by the wind, encircling the body of the martyr. He was there in the center of it, not like burning flesh, but like baking bread or like gold and silver being refined in a furnace. For we perceived such a sweet aroma like the smell of incense or some other precious spice.

Eventually, when those lawless men realized that his body could not be consumed by fire, they ordered the executioner to go up to him and stab him with a dagger. When he did this, a dove along with a large quantity of blood came out, so that the fire was extinguished.

*The entire crowd was astonished that there would be such a differ-
ence between unbelievers and the elect. Certainly he was one of the
elect, the marvelous Polycarp, who during the time he was among
us proved to be an apostolic and prophetic teacher and bishop of the
true church in Smyrna. For every word that came out of his mouth
was fulfilled and will be fulfilled.*

"That's amazing," said Artemidorus. "You have done a magnificent job of portraying Polycarp's endurance in the face of death
as being in accordance with the gospel. But that isn't where it finishes, is it?"

"That's all we've written so far," replied Bourrus, "though we're
considering adding a bit more. We want to explain the conflict
over Polycarp's body, include some details about how he ended up
being cremated, and clarify why we only had bones to collect after
his death. We know that readers in other locations will want to
know what happened to his body."

"Yes, I imagine they will," agreed Rufina.

"We also plan to recommend that churches include a day to
commemorate Polycarp on the anniversary of his death each year."

"I like that idea," said Tavia. "I will never, ever forget Polycarp.
But others who didn't know him could easily forget. A celebration
day would be a good way to remember both his life and death."

"We also plan to instruct the Philomelians to distribute this
account of Polycarp's death to others who live farther away," said
Bourrus. "It wouldn't surprise me at all to learn that in the future
this writing became an important source of encouragement for
those who face suffering and the possibility of death for the sake
of Christ. I fully expect that God will use the account of Polycarp's
death to further the work of God's kingdom and to spread the glorious message of the gospel to the four corners of the earth."

All agreed. How could it be otherwise?

Conclusion:

This was the account of the blessed Polycarp. Although he was the twelfth person martyred in Smyrna (when those from Philadelphia are included), he alone is remembered by all—so that he is spoken of everywhere, even by pagans. He was not only a distinguished teacher, but also an outstanding martyr, whose martyrdom everyone desires to imitate since it was in accordance with the gospel of Christ. By his endurance he defeated the unjust magistrate and so received the crown of immortality. He is now rejoicing with the apostles and all the righteous ones, glorifying the almighty God and Father, and blessing our Lord Jesus Christ—the savior of our souls, the helmsman of our bodies, and the shepherd of the true church throughout the world.

Historical and Literary Notes

THE FOLLOWING NOTES WILL help readers sort out what is historical from what is fictional in this story.

Notes on the Prologue

page 1—*From the church of God residing as foreigners in Smyrna, to the church of God residing as foreigners in Philomelium:* The prologue begins as an adaption of the first words of *Martyrdom of Polycarp* and draws upon its style.

page 1—*true church:* I have decided to translate the expression that is usually simply transliterated as "catholic" (καθολική) when combined with the word "church" (ἐκκλησία) as "true church" wherever it appears in my translations (Ignatius, *To the Smyrnaeans* 8.2; *Martyrdom of Polycarp* 1.1; 8.1; 16.2; 19.2), and thereby highlight that this expression often functioned to contrast this variety of Christians from others claiming the Christian name.

page 1—*Germanicus . . . , shouting to the officials to get rid of the "atheists" . . . , and . . . find Polycarp:* The death of Germanicus, the statement "away with the atheists!" and the call of the crowd to find Polycarp are all found in chapter 3 of *Martyrdom of Polycarp.*

page 1—*So he withdrew to a small country house not far from Smyrna and remained for less than a week:* The setting for the book and multiple details in the narrative are suggested by chapters 5–6 of *Martyrdom of Polycarp*, including that Polycarp wanted to remain in Smyrna, that the Christians in Smyrna convinced him to go to a country house, and that Polycarp spent large amounts of time in prayer while in that country house.

page 1—*with a few companions:* We know that others stayed in the country house with Polycarp, since *Martyrdom of Polycarp* 5.1–2 mentions that there were others (plural) with him.

page 2—*So we took every opportunity to dialogue with our dear bishop:* It can safely be assumed that many Christians would have wanted to talk to the elderly Polycarp about his life as a Christian leader, his connections to the early Christian movement, and about whatever he knew about the successes and challenges of Christianity during his lifetime. Polycarp was uniquely situated to be able to answer many questions people would have had about the first and second centuries of the existence of the Christian church, as has been noted by many scholars. There were doubtless conversations during the days Polycarp spent in the house in the country, but the content of those conversations is unknown. We also do not know how many people were with him in this house.

page 2—*A deaconess in the church in Smyrna:* For evidence of women deacons in this period, note the comment in *The Letter of Pliny to Trajan* (about A.D. 112) that the two slave women he interrogated were known as deaconesses. Perhaps also relevant is Hermas, *Vision* 2.4.3 where Grapte is a woman who was assigned the role of instructing the widows and orphans—even though she is not explicitly called a deacon.

Character names

All the names used in this book are borrowed from people who lived in Smyrna in the 2nd or 3rd centuries A.D.

- *Bourrus*: He was sent by the Smyrnaeans and the Ephesians to travel along with Ignatius as a support to him and to act as his scribe when Ignatius wrote letters back to the Philadelphians and the Smyrnaeans (and Polycarp) after he passed through Smyrna. See Ignatius's letters *To the Ephesians* 2.1; *To the Philadelphians* 11.2; and *To the Smyrnaeans* 12.1. The language of *To the Ephesians* 2.1 where Ignatius calls Bourrus "your deacon/servant" suggests that he may have come from Ephesus, even though he was sent as a representative of both Ephesus and Smyrna. Assuming that he was a young man when Ignatius passed through, I have placed him in his early sixties in the book. Bourrus's character is the only real character besides Polycarp that we know anything about, and what we know about him is thin. This narrative imagines that he is still living 35–45 years after the period he appears, that he became an elder in the church of Smyrna, that he married a woman named Rufina, and that he was the owner of a country house on the outskirts of Smyrna.

- Rufina: Her name is drawn from a synagogue inscription from Smyrna dated no later than the 3rd century A.D. Her namesake in this story has no connection with the Jewish woman listed in the inscription.

- Tavia: Her name appears in Ignatius's letter To the Smyrnaeans 13.2. Some copies of our text read Gavia instead of Tavia. The real Gavia/Tavia is described as having a household, so was probably already getting up in years when she was mentioned by Ignatius, and thus very likely had passed away by the time of our narrative, set as it is just before Polycarp's death. And, of course, we have no idea whether she could cook! In our story, Tavia is a deaconess. On women deacons in the second century, see comments above.

- *Artemidorus:* His name is borrowed from a Christian man's name found among the graffiti in Izmir, dating from the 2nd or 3rd century A.D. One of the Turkish archeologists responsible for uncovering this graffiti, Cumhur Tanrıver, writes the following: "A group among the Smyrna graffiti can be connected [sic] early Christianity. First graffito reads 'of Artemidoros from Smyrna' and then 'Equal in value / Lord: 800, faith: 800.' Possibly two separate inscriptions but in the same hand. The collocation of 'lord' and 'faith' and the emphasis on their equal value is inescapably Christian." Cumhur Tanrıver, "Inscriptions and Graffiti in Smyrnaean Agora," (Evangelical Theological Society Annual Meeting, Atlanta, Georgia, Nov 17, 2015): 3. We know nothing more about the actual Artemidorus. I have simply decided to borrow the name of a Christian man who lived roughly in the period of Polycarp or shortly thereafter.

- Crocus: His name was also found in the graffiti uncovered in Smyrna. Nothing more is known about him except that he wrote his name on a wall in Smyrna at some time in the 2nd or 3rd century A.D. In our story, he is Polycarp's great–nephew, the grandson of Polycarp's sister. In reality we have no idea whether Polycarp had a sister.

- Anthousa: Her name was one of the names suggested (though not explicitly written) by a combination of numbers found among the graffiti at Smyrna.

- Alce: Her name appears as one of the women greeted by Ignatius in his letter To the Smyrnaeans 13.2 and To Polycarp 8.3. This might be the same Alce mentioned many decades later in *Martyrdom of Polycarp* 17.2, though there is no way to be certain. There is no intended connection between the real Alce (or Alces if there were two) and the character in our story apart from the fact that there were one or two real Christian women named Alce living in Smyrna at some point(s) in Polycarp's life.

Notes on Chapter 1:
The Period of the Apostolic Fathers

The order of the chapters is aimed to be roughly chronological, though the dating of most of these documents is difficult, and virtually all their dates are disputed. Our narrative starts with an overview of the entire period, and then moves to what may be the earliest document (though disputed), 1 *Clement*, often dated to around A.D. 95. The narrative ends with what may be the latest document (though that, too, is disputed), *Martyrdom of Polycarp*. Polycarp's martyrdom is often dated to around A.D. 156, and the document describing his death appears to have been written shortly after the event (though all this, too, has been disputed).

page 5—*on a donkey:* Polycarp was later transported on a donkey by those who arrested him, so it would not be surprising if the manner in which the elderly Polycarp came to the first country house and then was transported to the second was on a donkey. See *Martyrdom of Polycarp* 8.1.

page 6—*Turtles live so long because they move so slowly:* a humorous comment made (in Turkish) by an elderly Turkish man to the author in 1993 in a city not far away from Smyrna (modern Izmir).

page 6—*I was introduced to the good news in my youth:* We actually know almost nothing about Polycarp's early years. At his death he said that for 86 years he had been serving Christ (*Martyrdom of Polycarp* 9.3). Some would argue that this means he was baptized as an infant, others that he was baptized sometime later and lived an exceedingly long life (the *Fragment on Polycarp* in the Harris Fragments gives his age as 104 years). A consensus date for his martyrdom is around A.D. 156, which would place his birth in A.D. 70 if he died at the age of 86, or in A.D. 52 if he died at the age of 104. Either way, he could have known disciples of Jesus, not to mention some apostles, which is what was claimed for him by Christians such as Irenaeus.

page 6—*Asia:* This is not a reference to the continent of Asia, as most people know it today, but to the Roman province of Asia during the time of this narrative (modern western Turkey). Historians usually refer to the ancient region as Asia Minor instead of Asia to avoid confusion with the continent of Asia. This region would have been home to many cities connected with the Apostolic Fathers, including Smyrna, Ephesus, Tralles, Magnesia, Philadelphia, Hierapolis, and Troas.

page 6—*Knowing that Jesus Christ is being proclaimed—in that I rejoice, as the blessed Paul wrote. And I will rejoice:* This allusion is to Paul's letter to the Philippians 1:18. That Polycarp knew Paul's letter to the Philippians is supported by the mention of Paul's letter-writing activity in his letter *To the Philippians* 3.2, and likely allusions in 5.2 to Philippians 1:27, in 9.2 to Philippians 2:16, and in 12.3 to Philippians 3:18. For the language of Polycarp referring to Paul as "blessed," see 3.2 and 11.3.

page 7—*including the loss of life of eleven of our own from Smyrna and Philadelphia:* Polycarp is listed as the twelfth person martyred among those from Smyrna and Philadelphia in *Martyrdom of Polycarp* 19.1. It is possible that some of them were martyred after Polycarp.

page 7—*But I remember the words of our Lord when he said, "Blessed are those who are persecuted for righteousness' sake, for theirs is the kingdom of God":* Polycarp alluded to this saying of Jesus as recorded in Matthew 5:10 in his letter *To the Philippians* 2.3.

page 7—*It doesn't help that the Jewish community in Smyrna is unhappy with our Christian groups:* See *Martyrdom of Polycarp* 12.2; 13.1; 17.2; 18.1. Note also Revelation 2:9–10.

page 8—*poor-ones:* The label "poor-ones" in this narrative is a place-holder for groups referred to by later writers as Ebionites (derived from the Aramaic word for "poor"). I conjectured in the narrative that they might have referred to themselves as poor-ones because Jesus taught that the kingdom of God belonged to the poor (so Luke 6:20).

page 8—*the poor-ones are mostly found in or near Palestine:* See Eusebius, *Onomasticon* 172.1–3, section on Genesis.

page 8—*knowing-ones:* The label "knowing-ones" in this narrative is a place-holder for various groups referred to by later writers as Gnostics. This label is appropriate since one of the key words shared among the various groups so labeled is the word "knowledge" (γνῶσις), from which the name Gnostics is derived. Valentinus was one influential Gnostic teacher.

page 11—*I know you, the first-born of Satan:* Polycarp's dialog with Marcion and an explanation for his strong words is recounted by Irenaeus in *Against Heresies* 3.3.4.

page 11—*nor even churches primarily comprised of former pagans:* Please note that the word "pagans" is being used in its technical sense to refer to those who adhere to the traditional polytheistic beliefs and practices of Greece and Rome, rather than in a broadly derogatory manner.

Notes on Chapter 2: First Clement

page 13—*There was a revolt:* The paragraph that starts with these words provides a reconstruction of the occasion of the letter that is plausible, but not certain in its details. All we actually know is that there was strife, and that, from the perspective of the church in Rome, a "revolt" had taken place in which the younger leaders in Corinth somehow took over (3.3; 44.3, 6; 47.6; 51.1). We also do not know for certain that the revolt was led by up-and-coming leaders from within the church, even though this would make more sense than that someone coming into the church from outside had led the revolt.

page 14—*The leadership in Rome also decided to send a delegation of a couple of their own elders to try to turn around the situation in Corinth*: See 63.3; 65.1.

page 15—*sixty years ago things were different than they are now . . . The church in Rome wasn't led by a governing bishop who directed the affairs of all the house groups in his own city*: One piece of evidence for this assertion is that the "bishop's office" (ἐπισκοπή) seems to have been filled by elders (πρεσβύτεροι) in 1 *Clement* 44:4–5, and there does not seem to be a distinction between a bishop and an elder in this passage. Nor is there any indication that there had been a single ruling bishop in Corinth before the "revolt"; rather there were elders who had been deposed. Ignatius's letter to Rome written a decade or two later is another piece of evidence. If Ignatius had known about a monarchial bishop, it seems more likely than not that he would have appealed to that bishop and to the congregation to listen to him, since he emphasized the role of the bishop so strongly in his other letters. One more piece of evidence comes from Hermas, also from Rome, who treated the leaders of the Roman church as a group of elders (*Vision* 2.4.3; 3.5.1; 3.9.7–10; *Parable* 9.27.2–3).

page 15—*Your [Polycarp's] recent expedition to Rome*: See comments in Irenaeus, *Against Heresies* 3.3.4 and Irenaeus's *Letter to Victor* as recorded in Eusebius, *Church History* 5.24.16–17 (for context see 5.24.11–18).

page 16—*Clement was at that time a leading elder among a group of elders who oversaw the affairs of the church in Rome*: I recognize that 1 *Clement* was not simply written by an individual. 1 *Clement* was sent as a letter from the church in Rome to the church in Corinth (1.1), but its style does have the feel of a single, or at least primary, author. Eusebius in *Church History* 4.23.11 refers to the author as "Clement" (but also claims that he was the third bishop of Rome, even though a monarchial bishopric does not yet seem to have been in place in Rome at this time). *Hermas, Vision* 2.4.3, in light of its Roman provenance and early date, may also mention the same person: "Then Clement will send it ['two little books' from Hermas] to the cities beyond, since that is his responsibility." References to "Clement" in this chapter do not presuppose that Clement is the same Clement mentioned by Eusebius and/or Hermas, even though it seems perhaps more likely than not to be the same Clement.

page 16—*the letter calls upon Christians in Corinth to submit to the will of God; they do not call on them to submit to the will of the Roman church leadership:* See 9.1; 13.3; 14.4; 56.1.

page 16—*He reminded them of the order and unity with which they had carried out their church affairs:* See 1.2—2.8.

page 17—*He did this early in the letter by reminding them of negative examples of envy and fighting from the past:* See 4.1–13.

page 17—*He also appealed to positive examples in the more recent past:* See 5.4–7.

page 17—*The use of positive types from the past:* Those listed in this paragraph include Noah (7.6; 9.4), Jonah (7.7), Abraham (10.1–7; 17.3–4; 31.2), Lot (11.1–2), Rahab (12.1–7), Elijah, Elisha, and Ezekiel (17.1), Job (17.3–4), David (18.1–17; cf. 4.13), Moses (43.1–6; cf. 4.10), and Esther (55.6).

page 17—*appealing to the natural order:* See 20.1–12.

page 17—*'the rule of our tradition' that was handed down to them:* See 7.2 (cf. 19.2; 51.2).

page 17—*He quoted larger sections of Scripture to substantiate his points, whether from the Psalms, from the narrative about Job, or from the Proverbs:* Compare 18.2–17 with Psalm 51; 22.1–7 with Psalm 34:11–17 and 19 (LXX 33:12–18 and 20); 39.3–9 with Job 4:16–18; 15:15; 4:19—5:5; 56.6–15 with Job 5:17–26; and 57.3–7 with Proverbs 1:23–33.

page 17—*Since Corinth could boast an unbroken line of tradition from the apostles to the present:* See 42.1–5; 44.1–6.

page 17—*directly connecting to the Apostle Paul's own warnings from forty years before in a letter Paul had written to them about schism:* See especially 47.1–4. Compare also 34.8 with 1 Corinthians 2:9; 37.5 with 1 Corinthians 12:14–26; 47.3 with 1 Corinthians 1:12; and 49.5 with 1 Corinthians 13:4–7.

page 18—*It is packed full of godly and wise counsel, often on topics that don't directly connect with the conflict in Corinth:* See 62.1–2 which makes it clear that one of the purposes of the letter was to write generally about things that are "useful for a virtuous life to walk in piety and righteousness."

page 18—*Clement also penned a beautiful and compelling prayer toward the end of the letter, a prayer I have used repeatedly:* See 59.3—61.3 for the prayer. We do not know whether Polycarp personally ever used this prayer, though Polycarp clearly had read 1 *Clement*. For evidence that Polycarp knew 1 *Clement*, compare Polycarp's *To the Philippians* 2.3 with 1 *Clement* 13.1b–2; *To the Philippians* 4.2 with 1 *Clement* 1.3 and 21.6; and *To the Philippians* 4.3 with 1 *Clement* 21.3.

page 18—*The two older mediators from Rome, Claudius Ephebus and Valerius Bito, as well as a younger man named Fortunatus, were able to reason with the Corinthians and persuaded many to place themselves under the older leadership whom God had appointed for them. The church ended up having to expel a couple of the troublemakers, but the church recovered from it:* These sentences are mostly speculation, though the names of the delegation from Rome are mentioned in 65.1. But is it more likely that a letter that became so well-known in the church received a positive or a negative response from the church to which it was written? Would the letter have become well-known and used in other churches if it had been repudiated in

Corinth and the mediators sent away? The wide circulation of the letter and the lack of comment about such a scenario by later writers make it more likely than not that it was received and that order was restored to the church. But we do not know for certain.

pages 19–20—*Excerpts from 1 Clement:* The excerpts that follow each chapter are original translations from Greek (or in a few cases from Latin) by the author based upon the Greek text of Michael W. Holmes, ed., *The Apostolic Fathers: Greek Texts and English Translations*, 3rd ed. (Grand Rapids: Baker Academic), 2007.

Notes on Chapter 3: The Letters of Ignatius

page 21—*Hello, Uncle Polycarp!* We do not know anything about Polycarp's relatives, but we do know that *Martyrdom of Polycarp* 6.2 says that he was betrayed by members of his own household (οἰκεῖοι). A member of a household does not have to be a blood relative; he only has to be attached to a family unit either biologically, through adoption, or by circumstances (such as slaves who served in a household, or freedpersons attached to a particular household). Crocus in this book is a fictional character portrayed as Polycarp's grand–nephew.

page 21—*Herod:* "Herod" is mentioned by name in *Martyrdom of Polycarp* 6.2; 8.2; cf. 21, the "chief constable" as I have labeled him, or simply the chief of police. Some interpreters have suggested that Herod's name is a fabrication of the authors of the narrative to make connections with the passion of Jesus. But in light of his role as chief constable rather than as a ruler or judge, a better explanation seems to be simply that his name was Herod (or less–likely, that the Christians in Smyrna nicknamed him "Herod"). This does not mean that a connection to Herod's presence in the trial of Jesus was lost on the authors of the *Martyrdom*. As to whether there was any familial connection of this man with the famous Herod family, there is no way to know.

page 21—*there is no fear in love, but perfect love casts out fear*: An allusion to 1 John 4:18. We can be confident that Polycarp knew 1 John; see his letter *To the Philippians* 7.1 for evidence that he knew 1 John.

page 23—*Quintus rashly offered himself for martyrdom*: The event about Quintus is described in *Martyrdom of Polycarp* 4, including the note, "This is why, brothers and sisters, we do not praise those who turn themselves in, since the gospel does not teach such."

page 23—*Bourrus knew Ignatius*: See comments about Bourrus in the notes on the prologue. A real Christian man named Bourrus did in fact come in contact with Ignatius.

page 24—*Ignatius . . . referred to these soldiers as 'leopards'*: See *To the Romans* 5.1.

page 24—*he was apprehensive about possible turmoil in the church back in Antioch now that they were bereft of their leader*: Notice Ignatius's relief when he later learned that peace had been restored, *To the Smyrnaeans* 11.2; *To Polycarp* 7.1.

page 24—*a group of representatives to intercept Ignatius in Smyrna*: The company from Ephesus included the bishop Onesimus, along with Bourrus, Crocus, Euplus, and Fronto (*To the Ephesians* 1.2—2.2). The company from Magnesia included Damas, a young bishop, along with Bassus, Apollonius, and Zotion (*To the Magnesians* 2.1). Polybius, the bishop from Tralles, also traveled to Smyrna to meet with Ignatius (*To the Trallians*, 1.1–2).

page 25—*Ignatius wanted everything that a Christian did . . . to be done under the leadership of the bishop*: See, for example, *To the Ephesians* 3.1—6.2; *To the Magnesians* 2.1—3.2;

6.1—7.1; 13.2; *To the Trallians* 2.1–2; 7.1–2; 13.2; also *To the Philadelphians* 7.2; *To the Smyrnaeans* 8.1—9.1.

page 25—*Ignatius dictated a heart–wrenching entreaty to the Christians in Rome, begging them not to use any connections they might have in an attempt to prevent him from being thrown to the wild beasts: To the Romans* 1.1—2.2; 4.1–3; 6.2–3.

page 25—*Parts of the letter to the Romans are difficult to read because of the graphic details he used to describe his anticipated fate:* See *To the Romans* 5.3.

page 25—*He alleged that only after he had become a prisoner on his way to execution did he really start to become a disciple:* See *To the Romans* 5.1, 3; *To the Trallians* 5.2; *To the Ephesians* 1.2; 3.1.

page 25—*I say 'we' because I was with them:* The presence of Bourrus on this part of the journey is confirmed by *To the Smyrnaeans* 12.1 and *To the Philadephians* 11.2. Concerning Philo, a deacon from Cilicia, and Rhaius Agathopus from Syria, see *To the Philadelphians* 11.1.

page 26—*He learned that the turmoil in Antioch had died down, and that the church was united:* See *To the Philadelphians* 10.1; *To the Smyrnaeans* 11.2; and *To Polycarp* 7.1. Ignatius received a message about peace returning to Antioch, and this helped to alleviate his anxiety. But we do not know whether the peace was a dying down of the persecution that accompanied Ignatius's arrest or whether it was a cessation of tensions in the church, a concern that might be reflected in Ignatius's insistence on obeying the bishop. Either way, it was good news that he received from his home church.

page 26—*adding up to seven letters in all that he composed on his way to Rome:* Note that there is a long scholarly discussion about whether there were more letters (called the "long recension") or even fewer than the seven letters mentioned in this book (called the "short recension").

Since the time of Lightfoot scholarly consensus has held that the "middle recension," that is, the letters mentioned in the narrative, are the seven genuine letters of Ignatius, though the consensus is still occasionally challenged. (Note that the textual history of *To the Romans* is different than that of the other six, even within the framework of the common middle recension view.)

page 26—*I [Bourrus] headed back to Smyrna with two letters in hand for that city and then over to Philadelphia to deliver their letter:* We actually don't know whether Bourrus continued with the band of prisoners after Troas (in which case the letters back to Smyrna and Philadelphia would have to have been carried by someone else). We do know that the troupe sailed suddenly from Troas to Neapolis (*To Polycarp* 8.1) and that Ignatius wrote these letters "though Bourrus" (*To the Philadelphians* 11.2; *To the Smyrnaeans* 12.1) along with a warm commendation of Bourrus, which may hint that Bourrus was going to deliver the letters himself.

page 26—*So Ignatius's appeals also strengthened the hands of Onesimus in Ephesus . . . of Damas in Magnesia . . . of Polybius in Tralles, and also of the quiet bishop of Philadelphia:* For Onesimus see *To the Ephesians* 3.2—6.2; for Damas see *To the Magnesians* 2.1—4.1, 6.1-7.2, and 12.1—13.2; for Polybius see *To the Trallians* 1.1—2.3 and 7.1-2; and for the quiet bishop of Philadelphia see *To the Philadelphians* 1.1-2 and 7.1-2.

page 27—*In his letters to the Magnesians and the Philadelphians he seemed most apprehensive about people who pushed Jewish practices upon others:* See *To the Magnesians* 8.1—10.3 and *To the Philadelphians* 6.1-2; 8.2.

pages 27-28—*The idea that Jesus only appeared to be crucified, rather than actually and really being crucified, was viewed by Ignatius as a destructive and dangerous teaching; he would have called it a 'heresy:* For Ignatius's use of the word "heresy," see *To the Ephesians* 6.2 and *To the Trallians* 6.1. The view Ignatius countered is usually referred to as "docetism." The word *docetism* is derived from a Greek word that would have appeared commonly in the arguments of its proponents (δοκέω), since such people claimed that Jesus only "appeared" or "seemed" to be crucified. For Ignatius's anti-docetic comments, see *To the Trallians* 9.1—11.2; *To the Smyrnaeans* 1.1—4.1 (perhaps also *To the Ephesians* 7.1–2).

page 28—*Instead, Ignatius assumed that the marks of the appointment from God should be self-evident in the bishop's godly demeanor* (see *To the Trallians* 3.2; *To the Philadelphians* 1.2), *in the way he shares the mind of Christ* (see *To the Ephesians* 3.2), *and in his truthful doctrinal affirmations about Jesus* (see *To the Ephesians* 6.2).

page 28—*Zosimus and Rufus:* Zosimus and Rufus are mentioned with admiration along with Ignatius in Polycarp, *To the Philippians* 9.1. We actually know nothing else about Zosimus and Rufus, but since they are linked with Ignatius in the same sentence and separated out from the mention of others in the Philippian congregation, it is a reasonable inference that they were also Christian prisoners being transported along with Ignatius to Rome. That there were other prisoners besides Ignatius in the band is implied by the plural "of those being killed" in Ignatius, *To the Ephesians* 12.2. Where these other Christian prisoners joined the group is impossible to say.

Notes on Chapter 4:
Polycarp's Letter to the Philippians

page 31—*Crescens and his sister:* See chapter 14 for Crescens and his sister.

page 31—*the Philippian church had welcomed Ignatius and the other Christians when they passed through their city:* See 1.1.

page 32—*we already had benefited from a collection of the letters of the Apostle Paul we kept in Smyrna:* In light of Polycarp's extensive use of Pauline materials, it is a reasonable inference that there was a complete, or almost complete, collection of the letters of Paul available to Polycarp in Smyrna. His use of Romans is almost certain in 6.2, and probable in 3.3 and 10.1. His use of 1 Corinthians is almost certain in 5.3 and 11.2, and probable in 3.3., 4.3, 10.1, and 11.4. His use of 2 Corinthians is almost certain in 4.1, and probable in 6.2. His use of Galatians is almost certain in 5.1, and probable in 3.3. His use of Ephesians is almost certain in 1.3, and probable in 12.1. His letter–writing activity to the Philippians is explicitly mentioned in 3.2, and his use of Philippians is probable in 5.2, 9.2, and 12.3. His use of 2 Thessalonians is probable in 11.3 and 11.4. His use of 1 Timothy is almost certain in 4.1. His use of 2 Timothy is almost certain in 9.2, and probable in 5.2. In light of the close historical connection between the three Pastoral Epistles, Titus should probably be assumed to be known to Polycarp, and because of the close connection of the Thessalonian letters, 1 Thessalonians should also probably be assumed to be known to him. This only leaves Colossians (and Philemon—but there would be little occasion for Polycarp to use Philemon!). What is truly surprising is not Polycarp's failure to mention a little letter like Colossians, but that in such a short span he employs so much of the Pauline material! It would seem reasonable, then, to suggest that Polycarp's Pauline collection was either complete or almost complete by the time Polycarp wrote his letter to the Philippians.

page 32—*I dictated a short letter that Crescens copied . . . headed north carrying their precious manuscript back to Philippi:* Note that it is possible that *per Crescentem* in 14.1 means

that Crescens was the letter carrier rather than the scribe.
I am working on the supposition that he was both.

page 32—*They wanted me to write them a real letter; not just a
cover letter to go along with Ignatius's letters:* I have tenta-
tively accepted the position of P.N. Harrison (*Polycarp's
Two Epistles to the Philippians* [Cambridge: Cambridge
University Press, 1936]) that the extant letter of Polycarp
to the Philippians is in fact two letters, one a cover letter
for the collection of Ignatius's letters, and the other a letter
for the church in Philippi. Harrison's two letter thesis has
been adopted by some modern scholars, but not by others.
I have little invested in this, and would have few concerns
if I later found out that it was a single letter, since I think
that Polycarp's longer letter to the Philippians was written
early as well (contra Harrison who dated the longer letter
later). But I have a slight leaning toward Harrison's two
letter position over the position that the letter is a unity.

page 33—*The decision by the Philippian Christians to acknowledge
Ignatius and other Christian prisoners was not well-received by locals:* This is an inference from the encouragement Polycarp gives to the Philippians about suffering.
We do not possess any actual documentation that connects the outward difficulties of the Philippians to the
passing through of Ignatius.

page 33—*the examples of . . . Ignatius, Zosimus, and Rufus, . . . the
apostles and their founder Paul:* See 9.1–2.

page 33—*I wanted to remind the Christians in Philippi also to be
imitators of their Lord when they suffered:* See 8.1–2; 9.2;
10.1.

pages 33–34—*Valens and his wife:* See 11.1–4.

pages 33–34—*warning against the love of money at a few points in
the letter:* See 2.2; 4.1–3; 5.2; 6.1 and 11.1–4.

page 34—*I counseled . . . not to treat the couple as enemies of the
church, but rather as sick and straying members:* See 11.4.

page 34—*A doctor tries medicine on an infection before he cuts off a limb . . . but . . . someone who burns his tongue while drinking hot milk will instinctively blow even on cold yogurt:* The first proverb was made up for this book. The proverb about yogurt and hot milk is a version of a modern proverb found in Greece and Turkey.

page 35—*As Paul wrote, we have received salvation by grace, not by works. Salvation is by the will of God through Jesus Christ:* See 1.2–3, quoting from Ephesians 2:5, 8–9.

page 35—*Do not judge . . . and blessed are the poor and those who are persecuted . . . theirs is the kingdom of God.* See 2.3 where there is likely a general dependence by Polycarp upon 1 *Clement* 13.1–2 for the fact but less for the form of the introductory formula and Polycarp's maxims. Note connections with Jesus' teachings as recorded in Matthew 7:1/Luke 6:37, Luke 6:20, and Matthew 5:10.

page 35—*to maintain a good standard of conduct among unbelievers* (see 10.2–3), *to avoid temptation* (see 5.3; 6.3), *to bear up under persecution* (see 8.2—9.2), *and to pray for kings and others in authority* (see 12.3).

page 35—*I mentioned [Paul] by name at three different points in the letter:* Polycarp mentioned Paul by name in 3.2, 9.1, and 11.2–3. Strictly speaking, he employed Paul's name four times, since he mentioned him twice in 11.2–3, but the last two appearances of Paul's name are contiguous, so I view it as three occasions.

page 36—*I quoted from the letter of the Apostle John who stated that anyone who denied Jesus' fleshly body was an antichrist and that anyone who denied the testimony of the cross was of the devil:* See 7.1, quoting 1 John 4:2–3 and 3:8. Polycarp's statements appear to be directed against docetists.

page 36—*wives* (see 4.2) . . . *widows* (see 4.3) . . . *deacons* (see 5.2) . . . *younger men and women* (see 5.3) . . . *elders* (6.1).

page 36—*But as I was writing the instructions to the elders, I switched mid-stream and started using the word "we":* Note the switch to "we" in 6.2–3. It is possible that Polycarp's focus has broadened to everyone in the church at this point in the letter, but it seems slightly more likely that Polycarp continued his instructions to elders all the way to the end of ch. 6, and employed "we" to include himself among the recipients. Note also that he never employed the word "bishop" in his letter.

page 37—*But they decided to combine . . . Polycarp's second letter to the Philippians . . . with Polycarp's little cover letter that he had sent along with the Ignatian letters:* We do not know that this happened; but this is a historical reconstruction to account for Harrison's two–letter theory, which may or may not be correct.

page 39—The final translated excerpt, 11.1–2, is only preserved in Latin. All others are from Greek.

Notes on Chapter 5: The Didache

page 41—*I know that you show respect . . . tell others to pray for governmental leaders:* See *To the Philippians* 12.3; cf. *Martyrdom of Polycarp* 10.2.

page 42—*There are only two ways, . . . one of life and one of death:* See 1.1.

page 42—*The idea [two ways teaching] is found in the blessings and curses section of the old covenant writings:* See, for example, Deuteronomy 30:15, 19–20; cf. Jeremiah 21:8; Proverbs 14:12; 16:25.

page 42—*Jesus himself contrasted the wide gate . . . with the narrow gate:* See Matthew 7:13–14. Note also the many similarities between *Didache* 1.1—6.2 and *Barnabas* 18.1—21.9. See comments in the narrative of chapter 8 of this book.

page 42—*a document I learned about when Ignatius came through:*
I actually have no idea when Polycarp first learned about
The Didache. The way I've described it in the narrative
makes it appear that the various sections of the document as we know it had already been put together before
the second decade of the second century, that is, before
Ignatius passed through Smyrna. This is not impossible,
but many scholars view the publication of the compos-
ite document to have occurred sometime later, even if
some of the parts hail from an earlier period. The title
The Didache is a shorthand version of *The Teaching of the
(Twelve) Apostles,* which is itself an abbreviation of *The
Teaching of the Lord to the Gentiles by the Twelve Apostles.*

page 43—*The ethical section in combination with the practical
church advice section—plus a bit of writing about the end
of the age:* This document divides into three sections:
1.1—6.2 the Two Ways, 6.3—15.4 about church practice,
16.1–8 a brief apocalyptic section.

page 43—*helping churches both in Syria and beyond:* A scholarly
consensus has formed around Syria for its provenance,
but really there is no way to be sure. It seems to reflect the
concerns of a Jewish–Christian community.

page 43—*genuine teachings of Jesus:* All these examples are found
in chapter 1. *Pray for your enemies,* Matthew 5:44; Luke
6:27-28. *Turn your cheek,* Matthew 5:39; Luke 6:29. *Go
two miles instead of one,* Matthew 5:41. *Give away your
tunic, not just your cloak,* Luke 6:29 (Matthew 5:40).

page 43—*the avoidance of magic and sorcery, and the refusal to
abort children or commit infanticide:* All these examples
are found in chapter 2.

page 44—*If you can bear the whole yoke of the Lord:* On keeping
the law, see 6.3.

page 44—*instructions about baptism:* Instructions about baptism
are mostly found in chapter 7. In 7.1 baptism is "in the

name of the Father and of the Son and of the Holy Spirit";
in 9.5 baptism is "into the name of the Lord."

page 44—*fasting:* See 8.1.

page 44—*prayers:* See 8.2–3.

page 45—*the Lord's Supper:* See 9.1—10.7.

page 45—*But the prophets can offer thanks any way they want:* See
10.7.

page 45—*Prophets . . . " Bourrus sighed. "Now that's an issue that
hasn't always been easy in our ministry in Smyrna . . . :*
There is no historical evidence of problems with prophets
in Smyrna before Polycarp's death, but the reader should
be reminded that the Montanist controversy, which high-
lighted the role of prophecy, is right around the corner,
so it would not be surprising if there were precursors to
that movement. It could be argued, as some have tried
to argue, that Quintus (*Martyrdom of Polycarp* 4) was a
Montanist because he is described as "a Phrygian recently
arrived from Phrygia," and Montanism found its early
home in Phrygia. But this observation may mean nothing more than that Quintus was a man who came from
Phrygia.

page 45—*not to despise prophetic utterances:* An allusion to 1 Thessalonians 5:20.

page 45—*instructions for how to handle Christian visitors who
claim to be prophets, apostles, or teachers:* See chapter 11.

pages 45-46—*others who aren't prophets who pass through town:*
See chapter 12.

page 46—*bishops and deacons:* See 15.1–2. The text does not explicitly say that bishops and deacons can be supported by
the church, but it is a natural inference from the comparison of honor given to both groups.

Notes on Chapter 6: Papias

page 50—*And worrying never added a single hour to a person's life:* An allusion to the teaching of Jesus, see Matthew 6:27.

pages 50–52—*Hierapolis:* See Eusebius, *Church History* 2.15; 3.31, 36; *Chronicle;* Codex Vaticanus Alexandrinus 14.

page 51—*he still occasionally made the trek out to Ephesus or Smyrna:* We do not know how often Papias and Polycarp may have come in contact with each other. But they lived only about 120 miles away from each other for decades. Ephesus and Smyrna were the two most likely places a Christian leader from Hierapolis such as Papias would have had occasion to visit.

page 51—*He didn't appreciate people who talked a lot . . . very focused on history:* See comments in Eusebius, *Church History* 3.39.

page 51—*He knew John:* I recognize that many scholars follow Eusebius in holding to the view that there were two Johns, that is, John the Apostle and a purported John the Elder, based upon the opinion of Eusebius. Nevertheless, those who hold that there were two Johns basically end up giving preference to Eusebius's fourth-century interpretation of Papias's text (*Church History* 3.39) over Irenaeus's statement at the end of the second century (*Against Heresies* 5.33.3–4) in which Irenaeus asserts that Papias (and Polycarp as well) knew John (by which Irenaeus apparently meant John the Apostle; note his earlier reference to John as "the disciple of the Lord"). Thus, in the section that Eusebius quotes and tries to interpret as pointing to two Johns, a better explanation is probably that Papias mentioned John twice because he was distinguishing between 1) those who died and 2) those who were still alive to consult with personally. John the Apostle belonged to both groups; that's why he was mentioned twice. It should also be kept in mind that Papias's eschatology really bothered Eusebius; he had reason to minimize Papias's credibility. There is no way to know how early the idea of two Johns originated. My guess, based upon the way Eusebius wrote—as though Eusebius were trying to exegete a text of Papias rather than pass on a tradition he had received—is that the two-Johns theory originated with Eusebius himself.

page 51—*a living and continuing voice*: Papias seems to have had some preference for information he could gather orally from the apostles or those who knew the apostles. See Papias's comment in Eusebius, *Church History* 3.39.

page 51—*a natural formation on the hills just below Hierapolis*: The modern Turkish name for the mineral deposit formations beside the ruins of Hierapolis is Pamukkale, which translates into English as "cotton castle" (*pamuk*=cotton; *kale*=castle). Knowing this helps to conjure up an image for those who have never had the opportunity to see this natural wonder.

page 52—*daughters of Philip*: The daughters of Philip are mentioned by Eusebius in *Church History* 3.30-31, though Eusebius seems confused as to whether Philip of Hierapolis is Philip the Apostle or Philip the Evangelist, and whether he had four daughters or three.

page 52—*Expositions of the Sayings of the Lord*: This is the title of Papias's tome as mentioned by Eusebius in *Church History* 3.36. Jerome refers to it as *An Exposition of the Sermons of the Lord* (*Explanatio Sermonum Domini*) in *On Illustrious Men* 18. Maximus the Confessor refers to it as *Expositions of the Lord* in *Scholia on Dionysius the Areopagite, On the Ecclesiastical Hierarchy*, chapters 2 and 7.

page 52—*Christians are increasingly employing the codex form*: Christians adopted the new technology of the day more rapidly than did their pagan or Jewish counterparts. A codex is a book, that is, separate pages bound together on one side.

pages 52–53—*gospel of Mark, gospel of Matthew:* See Papias in Eusebius, *Church History* 3.39.

page 53—*Those who live until those times will see:* This purported saying of Jesus is recorded by Papias according to Irenaeus, *Against Heresies,* 5.33.4.

page 53—*Barsabbas . . . drank snake poison:* Eusebius, *Church History* 3.39; Philip of Side, *Explanation of the Lord's Sentences,* fragment 6.

page 54—*Papias and I disagreed about some details of how the future will unfold, though . . . we agreed that God will raise us up from the dead as he promised and that we will also reign with him.* This wording is derived from Polycarp, *To the Philippians* 5.2.

page 54—*Papias and I disagreed on whether there will be a literal millennium at the end of the age:* In this assertion I simply follow the lead of Charles E. Hill, *From the Lost Teaching of Polycarp,* WUNT 186 (Tübingen: Mohr Siebeck, 2006), 83–85 who argued that the early Irenaeus, following the "apostolic presbyter" whom he identified as Polycarp, did not accept a literal millennium, but that the later Irenaeus changed his own mind, accepted the position of Papias rather than that of Polycarp, and thereby came to accept a future literal millennium.

page 54—*Every vine would produce ten thousand shoots:* See Irenaeus, *Against Heresies* 5.33.3–4 for the details in this paragraph. Technically, these are the millennial views of Irenaeus, not Papias. But since Irenaeus is describing his beliefs as mediated by those before him, and since Papias is the best-known millenarian from the period before Irenaeus, it is reasonable to assume that Irenaeus also represents Papias's views in this section.

page 57—The final translated excerpt of Papias (in *Irenaeus, Against Heresies* 5.33.3–4) is only preserved in Latin. All others are in Greek.

Notes on Chapter 7: The Shepherd of Hermas

page 58—*my pillow burst into flames:* See *Martyrdom of Polycarp* 5.2 for Polycarp's vision of the burning pillow.

page 59—*We need to hold tightly and without wavering to our hope:* This is a paraphrase and condensation of Polycarp's own words found in *To the Philippians* 8.1–2, written for a different time and occasion.

page 60—*I have reservations about some aspects of this writing:* We do not know what Polycarp's opinions would have been about *The Shepherd of Hermas,* if he knew the document. It is difficult to believe that Polycarp would have been wholly opposed to this document since it was used once, seemingly as Scripture, by Irenaeus in *Against Heresies* 4.20.2 (citing *Commandment* 1.1). I think it unlikely that Irenaeus would have viewed it quite so positively if he had known that Polycarp was negative toward it. Of course, there is no way to know whether he had ever heard Polycarp mention Hermas. But it is also reasonable to consider the possibility that as a defender of doctrine, Polycarp might have had some questions about some of the teachings in the document, and some of that possible hesitation is represented in the narrative.

page 60—*Hermas was a prophet who lived in Rome:* See *Vision* 1.1.1; 4.1.2. The *Muratorian Fragment* also places him in Rome.

page 60—*His early ministry overlapped with the time of Clement:* See *Vision* 2.4.3. It is possible that this is not the same Clement as associated with 1 *Clement,* but perhaps more likely than not that it is the same Clement.

page 60—*Hermas never in his writings referred to himself as a prophet, even though he wanted Christians to receive his revelations as true—in contrast to those he counted as false* prophets: See discussion of false prophets in *Commandment* 11.

page 61—*But Hermas actually released his revelations in three stages—at least in their written form:* The paragraph in which this sentence is found is a reconstruction of how the various visions, commandments, and parables may have come together into a literary whole.

page 61—*he wasn't in leadership:* Hints that Hermas did not hold an official leadership position in Rome are found in his reticence to assert his own authority and the lack of other indicators that he was such a leader. See *Vision* 3.3.1; *Commandment* 4.2.1; *Parable* 5.4.2.

page 61—*his home life:* See *Vision* 1.3.1–2; 2.2.2–3; 2.3.1.

page 62—*the church is compared to a fine lady* (see *Vision* 1.1.5–6) *. . . an old woman changes into a more youthful woman* (see *Vision* 3.11–13) *. . . the church speaks in the voice of a mother instructing her children* (see Vision 3.9.1), *but in another is compared to a virgin who is morally pure at her wedding* (see *Vision* 4.2.1).

page 62—*parable of the tower:* See *Parable* 9.

page 62—*He had to wrestle through what to do with a sin he had personally committed after he had been converted and baptized:* See *Vision* 1.

page 63—*sin after baptism could be forgiven as long as the one who had sinned repented—but once, and only once:* See *Commandment* 4.1.8; 4.3.6. But compare *Parable* 8.10.1–2 and 8.11.1–5.

page 63—*I [Polycarp] do not believe that this can only happen once:* Polycarp himself seems not to have agreed with the idea of one-time-after-baptism repentance. In his *Letter to the Philippians* 11.4 he is hopeful that God will grant Valens and his wife true repentance, and makes no mention that it can only happen once. In 6.1–2 he asserts that "we are all in debt with regard to sin," and goes on to say that "if we ask the Lord to forgive us, then we ourselves ought to forgive . . . " In 2.1 he challenges the Philippians with the words: "leaving behind the empty and meaningless talk and the error of the crowd . . . " And even though he considered the docetists of 7.1 to be outside of the faith, in 7.2 he exhorts those who had been drawn into such teaching with: "let us return to the word delivered to us from the beginning."

page 64—*[Hermas] implies that God chose to put the Holy Spirit within the man Jesus on account of the holy and chaste life Jesus had lived on earth to that point:* See Parable 5.6.4–8.

page 64—*The rich . . . the poor:* See *Parable* 2 especially, but also *Parable* 1.11; 6.4–5.

page 65—*double-mindedness:* See especially *Commandment* 9.

Notes on Chapter 8: The Letter of Barnabas

page 70—*the helpers of our faith are reverence and patience, and our allies are endurance and self-control:* See 2.2.

page 70—*Barnabas of Alexandria:* This label for the author could justifiably be disputed on two counts. It is not certain that the letter was written in Alexandria, though in light of its affinities with biblical interpretation often associated with Alexandria (allegorical interpretation in particular), and the favorable use of this document by Clement of Alexandria (late 2nd to early 3rd century), locating it in Alexandria has won favor with many scholars. What about "Barnabas"? In some of our manuscripts, there is a title that includes the name of Barnabas at the beginning of the document; in others a title that includes the name of Barnabas at the end of the document; and in others no mention of the name of Barnabas. This leaves us with the following four options: 1) The letter was written by the

Barnabas who was a companion of Paul, as Clement of Alexandria and a few others thought, 2) It was pseudonymously written in this Barnabas's name to try to give the writing credibility, 3) There was another person named Barnabas who wrote it, 4) It was originally written without a name on it, and someone later added Barnabas's name for credibility. Of these, almost no one thinks it was written by the companion of Paul, leaving any of the other three as options. For the narrative I have decided to go with the position that it was written by someone named Barnabas who is otherwise unknown in history (perhaps a Christian named by his parents after the earlier Barnabas), although I think it equally likely that the appellation was added later, in which case it should be viewed as anonymous. If anonymous, then Polycarp would not have referred to the author by the name of Barnabas as he does in this narrative.

page 70—*His letter was written about twenty years ago around the time that Hadrian was building a temple to Jupiter in Jerusalem on the site of the destroyed Jewish temple:* A date of sometime in the 130s, shortly before or after the rebellion is derived by comparing 16.3–4 with Cassius Dio, *Roman History* 69.12.1–2 (compare Eusebius, *Church History* 4.6.4).

page 70—*that their faith would not stand alone, but instead would be accompanied by perfect knowledge:* See 1.5.

page 71—*the knowing-ones are making headway in Egypt right now:* The documents found at Nag Hammadi, most of which are Gnostic to some degree, are the main source of evidence that Gnostics were active in Egypt.

page 71—*the letter of Barnabas of Alexandria is not one of the writings of the knowing-ones because Barnabas openly shares his knowledge with everyone who will receive it:* See 17.1–2.

pages 71–72—*Clement is a good example of someone who interpreted the Scriptures historically for the most part, which for him included typological interpretation:* Even though Clement usually focused more upon historical patterns of comparison (typology), he also sometimes dipped into allegorical interpretations, as with his comment in 12.7 about Rahab's "scarlet thread" (cf. Joshua 2:18) which he saw as foreshadowing redemption through Jesus' blood.

page 72—*The allegorist assumes that . . . there must be . . . deeper meanings that were put there by God for us to find:* See 6.10–13. Notice that Barnabas says that these were spoken to "us."

pages 72–73—*laws given about such animals by Moses . . . require a spiritual interpretation, that is, an allegorical one:* See chapter 10 for his allegorical interpretation of food laws.

page 73—*Barnabas . . . was constrained by the tradition he had received:* See 1.5.

page 73—*He was also restrained by the Christian's hope for the future, by ethical boundaries for what constituted righteous living, and by love:* See 1.6.

page 73—*believed that God had endowed Christians with special insight and understanding . . . which allowed Christians like him to look back on events and laws to discern their spiritual interpretations:* See 6.10 and 10.12.

page 74—*those of us who don't [interpret allegorically]:* There is no example of allegorical interpretation in Polycarp's letter *To the Philippians*, but Polycarp (if the apostolic presbyter in Irenaeus is Polycarp), interprets the exodus from Egypt as a type foreshadowing the Christian's true exodus, that is, the coming to faith of Gentiles (Irenaeus, *Against Heresies* 4.30.1). Also, it is claimed by Irenaeus that he encouraged people to "search for a type" in the Scriptures (*Against Heresies* 4.31.1). The reader should be aware that there is a fuzzy border between typological interpretation and allegorical interpretation, though it is still useful to draw the distinctions mentioned in the narrative.

page 74—*Barnabas's letter ends with a discussion of the two ways . . . like the document from Syria:* The similarities between *Barnabas* 18–20 and *Didache* 1–5 are unmistakable, giving rise to a discussion of whether one document is dependent upon the other, or whether they both depend upon an earlier shared tradition.

Notes on Chapter 9: Second Clement

page 78—*To the only invisible God:* The quote that starts this chapter is from 20.5, the final sentence of 2 *Clement.*

page 79—*I don't actually know the name of the elder who spoke it:* It is possible, though not at all certain, that the historical Polycarp would have known who the preacher of this sermon was, if he knew the writing, which is not certain. Because of the style and the way Scripture is used, it is unlikely that the sermon was written by the same author who wrote 1 *Clement.*

page 79—*Bourrus, do you have any recollection of where we acquired the copy we have in Smyrna?* We really do not know the origin of this letter. The four main suggestions for its provenance are Rome, Corinth, Syria, and Egypt. A marginal preference for Rome or Corinth over the other two would seem appropriate because in all three extant manuscripts, 2 *Clement* appears together with 1 *Clement,* which was written from Rome to Corinth. It can be assumed that a copy of 1 *Clement* existed in both Rome and Corinth during the early second century.

page 79—*A scribe in Corinth copied the sermon . . . at the same time [as 1 Clement]:* We have no evidence that the church in Smyrna ever requested a copy of 1 *Clement* from the church in Corinth, but such a request might explain how the two documents came to be associated with each other.

page 79—*they worshiped objects made out of stones, wood, gold, silver, and brass:* See 1.6 for support that the sermon was addressed to Christians from a pagan rather than a Jewish background.

page 79—*There is one section in the sermon that suggests it was delivered at a special meeting of believers from various house churches who came together to hear messages from several elders:* This reconstruction is based upon 17.3, which mentions the admonishment of elders (plural), the comment about returning home, and the admonishment to meet together more frequently. Admittedly, this sentence could be read as envisioning a regular church meeting, but such a scenario might not explain the amount of work required to write down a sermon of this size.

page 79—*it was written down before it was spoken:* In 19.1 the preacher says, "I am reading you an exhortation that you might pay attention to what is written."

page 80—*The sermon focuses upon repentance and self-control:* See the summary statement in 15.1 for both of these themes.

page 80—*repeatedly focusing his messsage upon the future:* This paragraph draws upon 6.3; 9.1; 9.6; 12.1; 16.3; 17.4; 17.6; 19.3–4.

pages 80–81—*to pay special attention to what had already been written:* See 19.1 and the numerous quotations from earlier literature throughout the sermon.

page 81—*three sources of authority:* There were three sources of authority for second-century Christians, as Polycarp commented in his letter *To the Philippians* 6.3: " . . . as he himself [*Christ*] commanded, as did the *apostles* who preached to us, and the *prophets* who announced ahead of time the coming of our Lord."

page 81—*the elder included a few sayings of the Lord I've never heard:* In addition to sayings of Jesus known from the four gospels, this sermon also contains a few purported sayings of Jesus not found in any of the four gospels. See 4.5; 5.2–4; 12.2.

page 81—*the preacher countered them [the Gnostics] at various moments in his sermon, even though he doesn't address them directly:* see 9.1–5 and 14.3–5.

page 82—*by grace . . . not of works:* Polycarp quoted Ephesians 2:5, 8–9 in *To the Philippians* 1.3.

page 82—*fasting is better than prayer, and . . . giving money to the poor is better than either fasting or prayer:* See 16.4.

page 82—*the preacher may simply have been assuming that his listeners knew that faith is included in repentance:* Possible evidence for this assertion might be 11.1; 17.5; 20.2, though the speaker of this sermon tended to exhort toward moral behavior.

page 82—*Crocus betrayed Polycarp:* Crocus, of course, is a fictional character in this story, portrayed as Polycarp's great nephew. *Martyrdom of Polycarp* 6.1–2 mentions that Polycarp was betrayed by members of his own household. Another possible reconstruction is that the two young slaves mentioned in this text, one of whom confessed under torture, were themselves members of Polycarp's household.

page 84—*help Polycarp with his sandals:* Note that *Martyrdom of Polycarp* 13.2 indicates that others normally helped Polycarp with his sandals.

Notes on Chapter 10: To Diognetus

page 87—*We must pray for kings:* The exhortation that starts this chapter is an adaptation of Polycarp's words in *To the Philippians* 12.3.

page 88—*The apology for Diognetus:* This writing might be better categorized among the writings of the apologists (such as

Aristides, Justin Martyr, Tatian, Athenagoras, Theophilus of Antioch) than as one of the Apostolic Fathers.

page 88—*Diognetus was probably someone of importance in society, perhaps a government official, or somehow connected to a powerful family*: The basis of this assertion is the use of "most excellent" (κράτιστε) in the address, a designation commonly used when addressing a person with higher social standing, often someone having significant political or social clout. Compare Acts 23:26; 24:3; 26:25; Josephus, *Against Apion* 1.1; Luke 1:3. Note that it is possible that Diognetus was only a hypothetical character, created by the author as a foil in order to explain Christianity to a wider audience, though in light of the particular questions addressed, it may be better to assume that he was a real person.

page 88—*What god do Christians believe in?* The list of questions found in this paragraph are all from chapter 1.

page 88—*I don't know who he [the author/speaker] was*: If this was composed before Polycarp's death (the date is unknown), and if Polycarp knew it well enough to discuss it, Polycarp probably also would have known who wrote it. But we do not know who the author was, nor can we be certain of its provenance, though Asia Minor has often been suggested. In the end we have to admit that there is no way to determine whether Polycarp knew *To Diognetus*.

page 89—*the document itself suggests that it was composed to be spoken—perhaps at some sort of gathering initiated by Diognetus*: See 1.2 which suggests that it was spoken rather than simply written. The suggestion that this was publicly spoken to Diognetus may have similarities to the sort of setting Polycarp envisioned when he made the following proposal to the proconsul in the stadium: "I am a Christian. Now if you want to learn the teaching of Christianity, appoint a day, and give me a proper hearing" (*Martyrdom of Polycarp* 10.1).

page 89—*That we're atheists because we don't sacrifice to their gods; that we eat human flesh and engage in sexual orgies at our love feasts; that we're trying to subvert the government:* See Athenagoras, *Plea Concerning the Christians* 3, Minucius Felix, *Octavius* 9, 30–31, and *The Letter from Vienna and Lyons* in Eusebius, *Church History* 5.1.14 for evidence that these types of accusations were sometimes leveled against Christians.

page 89—*the speaker of this document sets out to answer a few of the misconceptions . . . and to recommend Christianity:* Many scholars view chapters 11–12 of *To Diognetus* as part of a separate document written by a different author than the one who wrote chapters 1–10, though some scholars argue for its unity. Since there is no unobtrusive way in the narrative to represent a possible division, the comments have been limited in this narrative introduction to chapters 1–10.

page 89—*reconsider whether the Greek gods . . . are anything at all.* See chapter 2.

page 90—*This sounds like a critique Isaiah or one of the other prophets would have made:* See, for example, Isaiah 44:10–19 for a similar type of critique in a different time and setting.

page 90—*The speaker argued that Christians are not like Jews in these matters:* See chapters 3–4.

page 90—*They are citizens of a different country:* On the distinctiveness of Christians, see chapters 5–6.

page 90—*The speaker compared Christians living in the world to a person's soul:* See 6.3.

page 91—*because we are an obstacle to people who want to indulge their pleasures:* See 6.5.

page 91—*The speaker compared what God did to a king sending his son:* The ideas found in the paragraph where this line appears are from chapter 7.

page 91—*Did the speaker explain how Diognetus could become a Christian?* See chapter 9 for how the author answered this question. See 8.6 for the final line of the paragraph.

page 91—*the speaker urged him to come to faith:* See chapter 10 for the content found in the paragraph where this line appears.

page 92—*I ask you, Father of our Lord Jesus Christ, that the eternal high priest:* The content of the prayer that follows these words is an adaptation of Polycarp's benediction in his *To the Philippians* 12.2.

Notes on Chapter 11: The Martyrdom of Polycarp

page 96—*since she was the one they forced to disclose our final location:* See 6.1—7.1. We do not know the name of the person who disclosed Polycarp's final location, only that it was disclosed by one of two slaves who was tortured for the information.

page 97—*I'll begin with Polycarp's response and read from there:* The first and longest excerpt in the chapter is translated from 5.1—16.2.

page 102—*We want to explain the conflict over Polycarp's body, include some details about how he ended up being cremated, and clarify why we only had bones to collect after his death:* See chapters 17–18.

page 102—*We also plan to instruct the Philomelians to distribute this account of Polycarp's death to others who live farther away:* See 20.1.

page 103—*Conclusion: This was the account of the blessed Polycarp.* The concluding excerpt is translated from 19.1–2.

Next Steps

THIS BOOK WAS WRITTEN to be a first-stop introduction, the simplest of all introductions for students wanting to get a taste of the Apostolic Fathers and a sense of the Christian movement in the first half of the second century. For next steps in studying the Apostolic Fathers I recommend the following three short introductions:

Paul Foster, ed., *The Writings of the Apostolic Fathers* (London: T & T Clark, 2007).
Clayton N. Jefford, *Reading the Apostolic Fathers: A Student's Introduction,* 2d. ed. (Grand Rapids: Baker, 2012).
Wilhelm Pratscher, ed., *The Apostolic Fathers: An Introduction* (Waco, Tex: Baylor University Press, 2010).

To study the texts themselves, be sure to pick up a copy of:

Michael W. Holmes, ed. and trans., *The Apostolic Fathers: Greek Texts and English Translations,* 3d. ed. (Grand Rapids: Baker Academic, 2007).
Holmes also includes brief introductions and bibliographies.

To learn more about Polycarp's life and writings, consult:

Paul Hartog, *Polycarp's* Epistle to the Philippians *and* The Martyrdom of Polycarp: *Introduction, Text and Commentary,* Oxford Apostolic Fathers (Oxford: Oxford University Press, 2013).

For even further steps in the study of the Apostolic Fathers, I recommend that you consult the bibliographies and sources cited in the footnotes and bibliographies of the volumes above.

Questions for Review

Chapter 1: The Period of the Apostolic Fathers

1. In the narrative, Polycarp mentioned two of his greatest joys as he looked back over his life. What were those joys?

2. In the narrative, Polycarp mentioned two of his greatest heartaches and difficulties. What were the two he mentioned?

3. Who were the poor-ones (Ebionites)? What were their beliefs?

4. Who were the knowing-ones (Gnostics)? What were their beliefs?

5. Who was Marcion? What were the beliefs of Marcion and his followers?

Chapter 2: 1 Clement

1. What took place in Corinth that gave rise to 1 *Clement* being written?

2. 1 *Clement* was written from where, by whom, to where, and to whom?

3. Though disputed, according to the narrative how were churches usually governed at the end of the first century when 1 *Clement* was penned?

4. What forms of persuasion were employed in 1 *Clement*? (There were quite a few mentioned in the narrative.)

Chapter 3: The Letters of Ignatius

1. Where did Ignatius call home? What were the circumstances under which Ignatius wrote his letters to the churches? Where was he headed?

2. To which churches did Ignatius write when the company stopped in Smyrna? To whom did he write during the stop in Troas?

3. What was the good news Ignatius received when he arrived in Troas?

4. What was one theme that Ignatius emphasized in all his letters (with the exception of his letter to Rome)?

5. What was different about Ignatius's letter to the church in Rome? What was his primary purpose in writing that letter?

6. Which two areas of false teaching did Ignatius seek to counteract in his letters?

Chapter 4: Polycarp's Letter to the Philippians

1. What two requests did the church in Philippi make of Polycarp of Smyrna?

2. What was the problem with Valens? What did Polycarp advise the church to do about Valens?

3. What kind of "righteousness" did Polycarp primarily address in this document?

4. How did the fact that Polycarp was writing to a church founded by Paul make a difference in how he wrote his letter?

Chapter 5: The Didache

1. Although it is difficult to be sure about how and where *The Didache* was composed, this narrative suggests a place and scenario proposed by many scholars. What is the scenario?

2. According to the narrative, are all the teachings in this document derived from Jesus' own teachings? Are some of them?

3. What instructions are given for how to do baptisms? Fastings? The Lord's Supper?

4. What instructions are given for how to deal with visiting prophets and teachers? What about Christian visitors who are not prophets?

5. Should the church financially support prophets and teachers? What about bishops and deacons?

6. How does this document conclude?

Chapter 6: Papias

1. Apart from leading the church in Hierapolis, what did Papias spend his time doing?

2. Where did Papias purportedly obtain the information he wrote down?

3. What do you find most intriguing in Papias's comments about the gospel of Mark? About the gospel of Matthew?

4. What were Papias's views about a millennium?

Chapter 7: The Shepherd of Hermas

1. Who was Hermas? Who was "the Shepherd?"

2. What are the three main divisions of the book? Did Hermas write all the sections of the book at the same time?

3. What were some of the images Hermas used for the church? What was he trying to communicate by employing these images?

4. What did Hermas believe about post–conversion sin and whether someone could repent and be restored?

5. Does the narrative suggest any areas of concerns with Hermas's doctrine?

Chapter 8: The Letter of Barnabas

1. Where and by whom does the narrative suggest *The Letter of Barnabas* was written? (Please consult the Literary and Historical Notes for more on the question of place and author.)

2. What was Barnabas's stated purpose for composing this letter?

3. What was Barnabas's approach to biblical interpretation? What is an example of his approach?

4. What were Barnabas's two keys that unlocked biblical interpretation?

5. How does the letter end? Is this final section similar to any other writings of the Apostolic Fathers?

Chapter 9: Second Clement

1. What kind of literature (genre) is 2 *Clement*? Does the narrative suggest that it was written by the same author as 1 *Clement* or by someone different?

2. What two themes are emphasized in this document?

3. How did the author go about trying to persuade his readers that they should emphasize these two themes?

4. When the author quoted from earlier literature, what were the sources of his quotations?

5. Does the narrative express any concern with this document's emphases?

Chapter 10: To Diognetus

1. What kind of literature (genre) is *To Diognetus*? Who does the narrative suggest Diognetus was? Who was the author/speaker of *To Diognetus*?

2. Why was this composed/spoken according to the narrative?

3. What does the author/speaker say about idols? What does the author/speaker say about Jewish practices?

4. According to the author/speaker, why do Christians receive abuse in the world?

5. What must Diognetus do to become a Christian according to this document?

Chapter 11: The Martyrdom of Polycarp

1. According to the narrative, what were the authors of *The Martyrdom of Polycarp* trying to communicate in retelling how he died?

2. Where was Polycarp hiding and how was he discovered?

3. Did Polycarp know ahead of time that he was going to be burned to death?

4. What did the authorities do to try to get Polycarp to recant?

5. What miracles are recorded as taking place at the time of Polycarp's death?

Thanks

THE FOLLOWING PEOPLE ARE due special thanks for their help on this book:

My wife, Trudi, and daughters, Ana and Grace, for talking with me about the characters and storyline. Grace also helped me work out the length of the book and what to include where.

Darian Lockett, for regular dialog about the second and third centuries, hermeneutics, and intertextuality.

Moyer Hubbard, for reading my manuscript and for interacting with me on some historical issues. Moyer has also modeled for me how to use narrative to teach history.

Paul Hartog, whose scholarly work on Polycarp has developed in some respects at the same time as my own, but who has surpassed me in many areas. I am grateful for the time he took to read my manuscript and to offer numerous helpful comments.

The students in my Spring 2016 Apostolic Fathers class at Talbot School of Theology of Biola University, and in particular, Jordan Cardenas and Brianna Smith for their comments and suggested edits.

My father, Drew Berding, for hundreds of sentence edits.

Denise Felli for reading the entire book and offering timely words of encouragement.

All those at Wipf and Stock who have helped me bring this book to publication, including Robin Parry, Brian Palmer, Matt Wimer, Jana Wipf, and the others whose names I do not know.

Of course, any errors that remain are my responsibility alone.

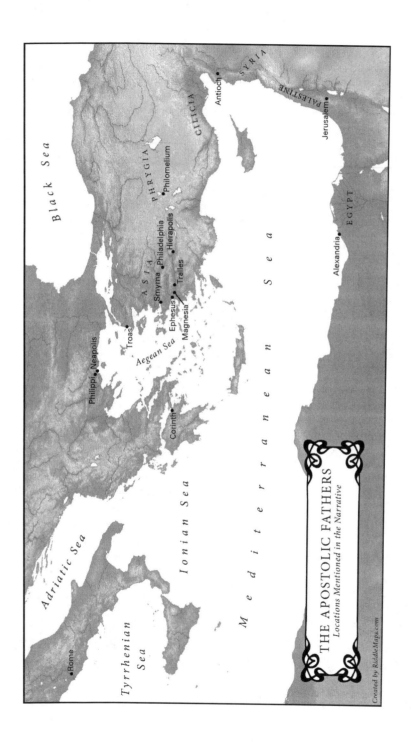

THE APOSTOLIC FATHERS
Locations Mentioned in the Narrative

Created by RiddleMaps.com

Other Writings by the Author on Polycarp and the Apostolic Fathers

Polycarp and Paul: An Analysis of Their Literary & Theological Relationship in Light of Polycarp's Use of Biblical and Extra-Biblical Literature. Supplements to Vigiliae Christianae 62 (Leiden: Brill, 2002).

"Polycarp of Smyrna's View of the Authorship of 1 and 2 Timothy," *Vigiliae Christianae* 53 (1999): 349–360.

"John or Paul? Who was Polycarp's Mentor?" *Tyndale Bulletin* 58 (2008): 135–143.

"Polycarp's Use of 1 *Clement*: An Assumption Reconsidered," *Journal of Early Christian Studies* 19 (2011): 127–139.

"Polycarp of Smyrna" in *The Encyclopedia of Ancient History*, ed. Roger Bagnall, Kai Brodersen, Craige Champion, Andrew Erskine, and Sabine Huebner (Wiley-Blackwell, 2013), 5396–5397.

"'Gifts' and Ministries in the Apostolic Fathers," *Westminster Theological Journal* 78 (2016): 135–158.